Formed
Holy
in
His Image

Spirit, Soul & Body

Gwen Ebner

ISBN-10: 1463773021
ISBN-13: 978-1463773021

Ebner, Gwen. *Formed Holy in His Image: Spirit, Soul and Body*. North Charleston, SC: CreateSpace, 2011.

I give glory to the potter

who is forming me,

the clay, into his

perfect design.

Acknowledgments

This book was not birthed alone; it involved a community of Christians who were also committed to growing in Christ. I want to express love and appreciation to my daughters, Shelley Hitz and Stacey Reeder, who are my best friends. We have spent hours talking about life and growth, learning from one another! Thanks to my sisters, Donna Toombs and Robin Barnett who have been on this journey with me for my whole lifetime and with whom I have shared many conversations. Thanks to my accountability partners, Connie Miller and Norma Walters, who have walked with me in this formational journey. We have grown together through thick and thin and our 7:00am bible studies have been a place of incubation and application for some of these ideas. Thanks also to Anita Patrick, a great friend, with whom I have discussed growth and wholeness issues.

A thank you to Jeannine Grimm who helped edit some of this material and with whom I have engaged in many hours of banter about many different subjects My thanks also goes to megan@msixdesign.com for designing the book cover for me. And finally, I want to express thanks to the "love of my life", my husband Chet who also helped me with some of the editing of this book. I am so grateful to be traveling with him on this journey toward being holy and whole. He and I love sharing these concepts with others.

In 2000 I began sharing these concepts with students, so in a sense, these words are partially a by-product of many class sessions and discussions. I want to express my appreciation for all the students who have been in my Ministerial Person classes. Your input has been invaluable. May you integrate these concepts into your life and ministry and stay on the path of wholeness as long as you live!

Again, I thank all of you for your contributions to this, God's work!

Contents

Introduction

In 2009 I wrote *Wholeness for Spiritual Leaders: Physical, Spiritual, and Emotional Self-Care* for a class I taught called Ministerial Person. My students began to tell me how the material was positively affecting them and that they believed it would be helpful for all Christians. One day I sensed God saying, "Create a resource that will enable the principles of physical, spiritual, and emotional wholeness to be used with individuals and groups in any setting."

So, here it is…adapted as a resource for all Christians, whether you are a leader or not. I pray that it will help you as you grow in Christ and are formed in every way. I have been, and still am, on this journey myself and know how much God has used these principles to form and transform me.

Jesus is our example in walking this journey. He exemplified a person who was mature in every way, "And Jesus grew in wisdom and stature and in favor with God and men."[1] He modeled this for his disciples and calls us to this kind of growth today! So, "we take our lead from Christ, who is the source of everything we do…His very breath and blood flow through us, nourishing us so that we will grow up healthy in God, robust in love."[2] He simplified all the laws and commandments into this directive, "Love the Lord your God with all your heart and with all your soul and with all your mind'…And the second is like it: 'Love your neighbor as yourself.'"[3]

Dallas Willard describes disciples of Jesus as "people who do not just profess certain views as their own but apply their growing understanding of life in the Kingdom of the

---

[1] Luke 2:52

[2] Eph. 4:13 [MSG].

[3] Matt. 22:37

heavens to *every aspect of their life* on earth."[4] Every aspect of life includes not only the spiritual, but also the emotional and physical – the spirit, soul, and body.

What would growth in this way really look like? The Scriptures give us direction concerning this process. "Offer your bodies as living sacrifices, holy and pleasing to God",[5] and care for your bodies with respect since they are the "temple of the Holy Spirit."[6] Instead of being conformed to the patterns of this world, you are to be transformed by the renewing of your mind.[7] In addition, continue working out your salvation with fear and trembling,[8] living a selfless, obedient life.[9] With God's strength demolish strongholds that have taken root within you,[10] as you replace Satan's lies with God's truth.[11] This will enable you to become your true self, taking off the false masks and the "fig leaves" you have used to cover your shame.[12]

Personal growth and formation has been an interest of mine for most of my adult life, but finding out how to involve my whole being in it has always been a challenge. It wasn't until I faced an over-whelming crisis in my life and found my need for God so great that I began a journey toward authentic

---

[4] Dallas Willard, *The Great Omission* (New York: Harper Collins, 2006), xi [italics added].

[5] Rom. 12:1

[6] I Cor. 6:19

[7] Rom. 12:2

[8] Phil. 2:12

[9] Phil. 2:5-8

[10] II Cor. 10:4-5

[11] Rom. 1:25

[12] Gen. 3:7

growth in all areas of my life. I have enjoyed discovering these truths in solitude as well as with family, friends, and students. It has been a joy to experience God's touch and transformation in all areas of my life.

It is my desire that you not only go on this journey yourself, but that you take someone along with you. I encourage you to use this resource in small groups, in bible studies, and in discipleship classes.

Using the Material

I have provided two exercises at the end of each part. I call them, "Going Deeper". The first section has reflection questions that can be used by individuals or small groups. The second section is called "Taking Time to be Formed". This section provides ways to continue applying this material for five days. If you are doing this in a small group, you can take a few moments of the next session to share what you have experienced as you completed these five days of formational experiences since you last met. Feel free to take more than one group session to cover some of the sections that need more discussion. This material cannot help you unless you apply it to your life. Formation takes time and happens best in community.

May those of you who read this book find more than just words. May you find a closer connection to the one to whom all words belong, the triune God - Father, Son, and Holy Spirit. For this journey is not possible without the love of our Creator, the sacrifice of Jesus, and the power of the Holy Spirit. I have come to realize that I am in control of very little. Therefore, my primary task in life is to love and obey God, surrendering to him each day as I walk on this journey toward an intimate relationship with him, the master potter.

So what will be your part in this formational journey? Jean-Pierre de Caussade sums it up with these words, "And so we leave God to act in everything, reserving for ourselves only love and obedience to the present moment."

"Personal change is not a clean, clear-cut process. Like clay whirled on a potter's wheel, God seems to offer repeated opportunities to change."
(Anonymous)

Be Aware!

God desires to make you holy and whole, but he is a potter who *will not force his will on you* even though you may suffer consequences for your choices!

> What sorrow awaits those who argue with their Creator. Does a clay pot argue with its maker? Does the clay dispute with the one who shapes it, saying, 'Stop, you're doing it wrong!' Does the pot exclaim, 'How clumsy can you be?'[13]

My prayer is that you will be pliable, workable, and willing clay in the master's hands as you go on this journey to be formed holy and whole in his image!

---

[13] Isa. 45:9 [NLT].

Part I

HOLY AND WHOLE

Long before he laid down earth's foundations, he had
us in mind, had settled on us as the focus of his love,
to be made *whole and holy* by his love.
-Ephesians 1:4[MSG][14]

Total health involves embracing our brokenness.
Wholeness should never be seen as perfection, but
rather an acknowledgment and acceptance of weakness.
-Roy Oswald

In Jeremiah 18 we find a potter making something at
his wheel but the jar he is forming does not turn out as he had
hoped, so the potter starts all over again using the same clay
"shaping it as seemed best to him".[15] Then God tells Jeremiah
to give this message to the house of Israel, "Can I not do with
you as this potter does? Like clay in the hand of the potter, so
are you in my hand."[16]

The picture on the front of this book is a poignant
reminder that we are the clay and "the work of his hand".[17] It
is the master potter who is forming us and hopefully we will
not respond as Israel did when the potter asked them to
straighten out their lives and yield to his hands. They replied
with these words, "Don't waste your breath. We will continue

---

[14] Italics added.

[15] Jer. 18:4

[16] Jer. 18:6

[17] Isa. 64:8

to live as we want to, stubbornly following our own evil desires."[18]

Being holy and whole will never happen unless we yield to the potter's hands. For "we ourselves are like fragile clay jars containing this great treasure. This makes it clear that our great power is from God, not from ourselves".[19]

---

[18] Jer. 18:12 [NLT].

[19] II Cor. 4:7 [NLT].

Chapter 1

A Biblical Understanding

God's intention, from the beginning, was for his people to be holy. "He chose us in him before the creation of the world to be holy and blameless in his sight."[20]Adam and Eve were created "holy and whole" but their sin of disobedience disrupted God's plan and consequently their relationship with him.

After that God chose another way to convey his intentions. He said to Moses, "Speak to the entire assembly of Israel and say to them: 'Be holy because I, the Lord your God, am holy.'"[21] God made it clear they could not do this by themselves, "I am the Lord, who makes you holy."[22] But when he offered them guidelines and laws to help them in this process, they either made the law their god or discarded the law and chose to serve other gods instead. God instructed them to offer the blood of animal sacrifices for the forgiveness of sin, but this had to be repeated over and over again because they continually failed to be holy. So "when the time had fully come, God sent his Son....to redeem those under the law."[23] "For Christ died for sins *once for all*, the righteous for the unrighteous, to bring [us] to God."[24] In response, we can offer our bodies to God as "living sacrifices, *holy* and pleasing to

---

[20] Eph. 1:4

[21] Lev. 19:2

[22] Lev. 20:7

[23] Gal. 4:5

[24] I Pet. 3:18 [italics added].

3

God" which becomes our "spiritual act of worship."[25] "For God did not call us to be impure, but to live a *holy* life."[26]

We see Paul's passion to be like Christ as he declares these words, "I want to know Christ and the power of his resurrection....becoming like him in his death.[27]" What was this power that Paul was talking about? The power that came from Christ's resurrection was "victory over sin" which allows us to be holy and pleasing to God. After all, if Christ had not been raised, our faith would be futile and we would still be in our sins.[28] Becoming like him in his death gives us the power to live a holy life but will involve a daily dying to ourselves. [29] And what will this "becoming like him" involve?

1. It will first involve believing in his name, forgiveness of sins and receiving him, enabling us to know Christ.[30] This allows us to be connected with the One who makes us holy. "Both the one who makes people holy and those who are made holy are of the same family."[31]

2. As His child we will then be challenged to deny ourselves, surrender, and submit to his will, allowing him to be in control of our lives. This is the sanctifying work of the Spirit that will move us toward being holy.[32]

---

[25] Rom. 12:1 [italics added].

[26] I Thess. 4:7 [italics added].

[27] Phil 3:10

[28] I Cor. 15:17

[29] I Cor. 15:31, Luke 9:23

[30] Jn. 1:12

[31] Heb. 2:11

[32] I Pet. 1:2

3. Being holy will also mean that we will be different than the world. Instead of being conformed to the pattern of this world, God will empower us to be transformed by the renewing of our minds.[33]

4. We will also need to suffer trials and problems, so that our "faith may be proved genuine"[34] and we may become "mature and complete, not lacking anything".[35] Paul was not content to just know Christ and the power of his resurrection; he wanted to also *know* the fellowship of sharing in his sufferings, becoming like him in his death.[36] He wanted to become a "living sacrifice, holy and pleasing to God."[37] This is a model on how to become holy.

But how does this connect, then, with being whole? If something is whole, it is entire and complete, implying that nothing had been omitted or ignored. When talking to the Christians at Thessalonica, Paul instructs these believers in this way, "May God himself, the God of peace, sanctify you through and through. May your whole spirit, soul and body be kept blameless at the coming of our Lord Jesus Christ."[38] When Paul uses the word "sanctify", he is implying a *process* of growth that will lead us to holiness, not an event or state of being. In his use of spirit, soul, and body, he is not referring so much to the distinct parts of a person as to the effect that this wholeness will have on those parts in relationship to one's

---

[33] Rom. 12:2

[34] I Pet. 1:6-7

[35] James 1:2-4

[36] Phil. 3:10

[37] Rom. 12:1

[38] I Thess. 5:23

5

entire being. This is his way of saying that God must be involved in *every* aspect of our lives, not in just part of our lives.

A growth toward wholeness is a "process", not a particular event that we experience. It is the "lived out experience" of everyday life that takes place in the power of the Holy Spirit, not in our own strength. It is often best developed as a result of trials we encounter, because trials test our faith, and in the process, develop perseverance in our lives. That perseverance must finish its work so that we may be *"mature* and *complete*, not lacking anything."[39]

The Greek word for mature is *teleios,* and denotes the end result of the growth process which is to be perfect, full-grown, and fully developed. Jesus also used the word teleios. It first occurs in his Sermon on the Mount when he says, "Therefore you shall be *perfect* (teleios), just as your Father in heaven is *perfect"* (teleios).[40] He also made use of this word when he told the rich young man, "If you want to be *perfect* (teleios), go, sell your possessions and give to the poor,"[41] herein meaning to be perfect in the sense that he would be truly obedient and fully devoted.

Being perfect and complete was not meant to imply that we would never sin, be tempted, or ever make a mistake again. Instead, it implies that nothing has been omitted or ignored. This is his way of saying that God must be involved in every aspect of our lives, not just in part of our lives, so that he can empower us to live like him in all of the circumstances of life.

The second word James uses is *holokleros*[42]. This is the Greek word for our English word complete and implies a

---

[39] James 1:4 [italics added].

[40] Matt. 5:48 [NKJ].

[41] Matt. 19:21

[42] James 1:4

6

meaning of being whole, complete in all its parts, perfect. This word is found in only one other place in the New Testament, in I Thess. 5:23 (quoted above) when Paul declares that their *whole* (holokleros) spirit and soul and body be preserved blameless. In the beginning of that verse Paul also combined the essence of teleios and holos with the Greek word, holoteles, which comes from holos (meaning whole) and teleo (meaning to bring to maturity or an end) as he prays that God "sanctify them *wholly*"(holoteles) or mature them in a holistic manner.

A theology of wholeness rests on a process of becoming what God calls us to be in *every aspect of our lives* in a way that becomes habitual and seemingly instinctive. This means the principles of God must progress from a "head knowing" to a "heart dwelling" as we accept God's principles as our very own. Jesus reminds us that it is from the overflow of the heart that the mouth speaks,[43] for the heart is the "wellspring of life".[44] Building God's principles within our heart will take practice, repetition, surrender, humility, and continuous growth in Christ one day at a time.

This process toward wholeness will not be immediate. It will require patience, born through trials, and a life lived in obedience to God. It will be the pursuit of one victorious day at a time until the sun sets on enough days to begin forming new habits. However, as we allow this process to work within our lives, we will grow to become more and more like Jesus - increasingly perfect, mature, full-grown, complete, whole, and holy. James reminds us that this process also has benefits beyond this life. "Blessed is the man who perseveres under trial, because when he has stood the test, he will receive the crown of life that God has promised to those who love him."[45]

---

[43] Matt. 12:34

[44] Prov. 4:23

[45] James 1:12

7

In Matthew 25:14-30 Jesus tells a story about a man who was going off on an extended trip. He calls his three servants together, delegates responsibilities and gives them various amounts of money to manage and invest. Each man will be held accountability upon the master's return for how he has managed and invested what was given to him.

This story lays out an important principle for kingdom living. God created everything and has entrusted us with the responsibility of caring for it. In other words, we are stewards of *his* possessions; they are not ours. We will be held accountable for how we have managed them and honored him with them. Even though this parable frames the resources as money, we know that it certainly applies to other things that we are entrusted with by God: possessions, time, talents, relationships, our body and our sexuality. "You do not belong to yourself, for God bought you with a high price."[46]

As you continue reading this book, looking at all areas of your life, remember that you are only stewards of everything you have. Nothing is yours; it all belongs to God. When you remember that, it changes everything! You will then need to know what the master wants you to do with this resource and how to best manage it...for him!

I grew up in a legalistic church environment. Spiritual growth was measured by external measures, such as, certain clothing restrictions, avoidance of particular behaviors, church attendance, and the approval of others. A wholeness that encompassed one's physical, emotional, and spiritual life was never taught. Overweight, poor eating habits, ungodly attitudes, gossip, and double standards were accepted as normal. Growing up in the church I rarely saw humility, meekness, mercy, selflessness, peacefulness, and dependence on God modeled. Because of the unpublished "do's and don'ts list" and the judgment that followed any failure to abide by it, I was left with a sense of shame and a lack of understanding of

---

[46] I Cor. 6:20 [NLT].

God's grace. I also failed to see the larger picture of what being holy and whole meant to God.

Consequently, I lived many years feeling distant from God and was emotionally starved and immature. In order to cope I began to try to order my physical life myself, trying to fix my lack of fulfillment by eating perfectly and following the "rules" of health. I was also constantly working in order to try to feel good about myself emotionally and to get "pats on the back". In addition, I became legalistic in my spiritual life, believing ritualistic habits would please God. Somehow I didn't realize the overall connection between my emotional, spiritual, and physical health. I was trying to fix life in my own way.

It wasn't until I experienced some difficult trials or what James refers to as the testing of my faith[47] that I began to grow in wholeness and maturity *(teleios)*. The trials brought me to a place of depending on God in a way I had never done before. When I began learning how to relax and live in God's peace, I found my physical body working better. I had less stomach problems and bowel disturbances, symptoms that had arisen from my challenged immune system. Gradually I let go of my anger, my control on life, and learned to trust God for the wholeness he had for me. Consequently, this created growth in my emotional health, as well as in my connection with God. These difficult trials had become the catalyst for helping me embrace God's grace and embark upon a journey of growth in every area of my life!

The word conversion may offer us further understanding regarding the process toward being holy and whole. E. Stanley Jones defines conversion as "the act of a moment and the work of a lifetime."[48] Jones' comment indicates that conversion is

---

[47] James 1:3

[48] E. Stanley Jones, *Conversion* (New York: Abingdon, 1959), 210.

not an end in itself, but is a continuous and lifelong process which "proceeds layer by layer, relationship by relationship, here a little, there a little – until the whole personality, intellect, feeling, and will have been recreated by God."[49] Richard Foster contends that conversion does not make us perfect, but it does "catapult us into a total experience of discipleship that affects - and infects – every sphere of our living. When we begin a pilgrimage of faith, we may not know all that conversion to Christ will mean, but we can be assured that no corner of our lives will be left untouched." [50]

Unfortunately, our churches are filled with people who are looking for sudden and painless paths to change and growth or what Dietrich Bonhoeffer calls "cheap grace." However, the process of conversion is not quick or painless; it costs us dearly. It involves a process of dying to one's self - a practice that is definitely countercultural and will involve the reordering of our *total* life.

We have a useful example of wholeness in Luke's description of the boy Jesus. "And Jesus grew in wisdom and stature, and in favor with God and men."[51] The word "grew" is an imperfect active indicative Greek verb which carries the meaning of a past continuous action. As an imperfect active indicative verb it not only means "he *was* growing" but also indicates that "he *is* growing" in a continuous manner. That should also be the pattern of our growth.

Jesus' manner of growth is noted in a number of aspects – wisdom, stature, favor with God and favor with men. Wisdom refers not only to practical wisdom but skill, knowledge, emotional maturity, and moral insight. Stature is a word that we associate with developmental growth and the

---

[49] Sue Monk Kidd, *When the Heart Waits: Spiritual Direction for Life's Sacred Questions* (New York: HarperCollins Publishers, 1990), 26.

[50] Richard J. Foster and James Bryan Smith, *Devotional Classics* (San Francisco: HarperCollins, 1993), 306.

[51] Luke 2:52

physical care and maintenance of our bodies. Favor refers in a general way to a favorable attitude toward another, resulting in approval and goodwill. The terms, favor with God and man, seem to indicate favorable growth in a personal relationship with God (spiritual growth) and in a personal relationship with human beings (relational growth).

When asked what it means to be formed in the image of God, most people focus primarily on spiritual aspects (Gen. 5:1; I Cor. 15:49; Eph. 4:24; I John 3:2). However, Luke 2:52 reminds us that growth is a process that encompasses all aspects of our life. God created us to be more than just a spiritual being. He wants to transform the entirety of our life – our spiritual essence, as well as our emotional being and physical bodies. All of these – spirit, soul, and body - work together and interact with one another. They all matter to God!

Jesus demonstrated the importance of our entire being (spirit, soul, and body) in the way he offered healing to people. When healing the paralytic in Matt. 9, Jesus frames it in a *spiritual* context, "Take heart, son; your sins are forgiven."[52] But when healing another paralytic by the pool of Bethesda, Jesus asks the man if he wants to get well and then gives the man a *physical* command, "Get up! Pick up your mat and walk."[53] Two paralytics are healed, but Jesus approaches their healing through different aspect of their being - one in a spiritual context and the other through a question and a physical command.

Other examples further demonstrate the variety of ways that Jesus offered restoration to people. When healing the man who is mute in Matt. 9:32-33, Jesus simply cast out the demon in him and the man who had been mute spoke. Jesus informs the woman with an issue of blood that her faith has made her

---

[52] Matt. 9:1-8

[53] Jn. 5:1-15

whole. And he adds, "Go in peace,"[54] words indicating an emotional aspect to her healing, especially significant to her due to the ostracizing and devaluing she had received for twelve years because she was considered "unclean." This reminds us that the various aspects of our being are connected to one another and that Christ knows exactly how to offer growth and healing to us if we will only submit to him and obey.

---

[54] Luke 8:42-48

Chapter 2

Traits of Character and Conduct

In the Beatitudes Jesus offers traits of character and conduct that can help us in our journey toward being holy and whole. Jesus actually claims that we will be "blest" when we live out our life according to these principles. However, this state of blessedness is not the result of favorable circumstances in life, but comes from being indwelt by Christ. The first seven of the nine Beatitudes seem to turn life wrong side out because they are the reverse of the perspective of this world.

The first trait[55] reminds us we are blessed when we are poor in spirit. The Greek word for "poverty" is *ptochos*. This indicates a helpless person or a person not sufficient within one's self. Jesus is pointing out that the first step toward wholeness is a realization of our own spiritual helplessness. As we realize how dependent we are on God, we begin to desire "less of us" and "more of Him" and view ourselves more accurately in relation to who God is. Often we don't experience being poor in spirit until we are emptied of ourselves or at the end of our rope. Frequently our own pride can hinder us from growing in this character trait.

The blessing in the second beatitude[56] is upon those who are deeply sad and sorrowful. The word mourn comes from the Greek *pentheo*. This is more than a hurried "I'm sorry" and envelopes deep and repentant sorrow for one's own sins. David spoke about this type of mourning, "For I know my transgressions, and my sin is ever before me."[57] Later in this chapter he says, "The sacrifices of God are a broken spirit; a

---

[55] Matt. 5:3

[56] Matt. 5:4

[57] Ps. 51:3 [ESV].

broken and contrite heart, O God, you will not despise."[58] In this instance, David had experienced a deep sense of mourning for his own sin and it has broken his heart.

This type of mourning also takes place in regard to the sins of others. We see this demonstrated by Jesus as he mourns for the people of Jerusalem.[59] True mourning and a feeling of deep emotional pain can drive us into God's arms when nothing else will. He is the only true comfort.

The trait of meekness[60] comes from the Greek word *praus* which means gentle and humble. A person who is meek is unselfish, unpretentious, and willing to see themselves as they really are. They are content with who they are – no more, no less. The meek person is gentle and mild about their own cause, though they may be a lion for God's cause. Instead of needing to have their own way, they can yield to the will of God and to others. Jesus models this twofold type of meekness in both the clearing of the temple[61] and when responding to his accusers.[62]

The fourth beatitude uses the phrase "those who hunger"[63] from the Greek (*hoi peinontes*), indicating a person who has an intense desire and a good appetite. The verse also includes the word, thirst, which is perhaps a stronger word, a matter of life and death. Note that the emphasis is not placed on the righteousness of a person, but on their hunger and thirst for that righteousness. In this case it is a hunger for a restored

---

[58] Ps. 51:17

[59] Luke 13:34

[60] Matt. 5:5

[61] Jn. 2:14-16

[62] Matt. 27:11-14; Luke 22:70; 23:3, 34

[63] Matt. 5:6

14

relationship with God and a desire for the actions that lead toward a covenant relationship with him.

We also see that the Greek verbs of hungering and thirsting take the accusative instead of the genitive, creating the meaning of *the whole thing*. In reality, most people are content with less than what God has for them. They may have honesty, morality, and respectability beyond question, yet lack sympathy for the needs of others. Or they may be willing to give others the shirt off their back, yet often lose their temper when things do not go their way. This beatitude assures us that our intense desires, strong appetite, and thirsting for righteousness can and will be satisfied by God and we do not need to settle for anything less.

Those who are merciful[64] (from the Greek *eleemon*) are persons of compassion. They are characterized by a caring attitude for those in misery. However, this does not mean that we just feel sorry for a person or we have an emotional wave of pity for them. This indicates that we experience things *together with* the other person, literally going through what they are going through. This type of sympathy is not given from the outside, but comes from a deliberate identification with the other person on the inside.

Sometimes we are so concerned with our own feelings that we fail to be truly merciful to the feelings of others. Martha[65] is an example of this type of good intentions. She was trying to be kind and merciful to Jesus, but failed to see things through His eyes, thinking her act of mercy was to serve him food. But with the agony of the cross only a few days away, Jesus' real need was for rest, peacefulness and companionship. Instead she hurried and scurried around, complaining about the actions of Mary, creating the very opposite of the real compassion that Jesus needed. If she could have been more sensitive to the care that Jesus really needed,

---

[64] Matt. 5:7

[65] Luke 10:38-42

she would have found herself cared for in the process. What an interesting paradox!

The "pure in heart"[66] is from the Greek word *hatharos*, meaning unmixed, unadulterated, unalloyed. This Beatitude could be reworded to say, "Blessed is the man whose motives are entirely unmixed, for that man shall see God." This demands from us the most exacting self-examination. As we consider this Beatitude, we may wish to ask ourselves these questions: When I give generously to a cause am I in anyway basking in the sunshine of my own self-approval or finding pleasure in the praise and thanks which I receive? Does my service come from selfless motives or from motives of self-display? Is my work done for Christ or for my own prestige? Is my prayer and Bible reading done in order to have company with God or in order to satisfy my own piety?

The final Beatitude of the seven offers a blessing to "peace-makers" (Greek word *eirenopoios*). Jesus is not speaking about people who *love peace* or have a peaceful disposition, but of people who actively intervene to *make peace*. In order to be a participant in making peace, one has to first have peace in their own heart and soul. And that peace is not something we can manufacture ourselves or obtain from the world; it comes only from Christ.[67] The highest task which a man can perform is to establish right relationships between man and man. This is what Jesus means when he speaks of peacemaking.

The Beatitudes serve as an important pattern for not only the way Jesus carried out his own life, but for the way we must live. As we read and saturate ourselves in the character of Jesus, found in the Biblical narrative in Matthew, Mark, Luke, and John, we become aware of how Jesus can serve as our example for becoming holy and whole.

---

[66] Matt. 5:8

[67] Jn. 14:27

Chapter 3

Check-Up

Taking time to do a physical, emotional, and spiritual check-up can be a helpful process. It is not enough to nurture our spiritual lives; we must be transformed in every aspect of our lives. Ask yourself: What facet of my life is being neglected in regard to being formed in Christ?

Take a look at these statements and make a check by the ones that presently apply to you.

SPIRITUAL:
- o I haven't been spending regular time with God
- o I am not able to hear God's voice guiding me throughout the day
- o When I read scripture, I fail to apply it to my life or fail to be obedient to what it is saying to me
- o I tend to want to run my life myself instead of allowing God to be in control
- o I know *of* God or *about* God, but I do not have a sense of his presence on a daily basis
- o I spend more time meeting my own needs (or the needs of my family) than the needs of others (sharing my resources with others, giving to the church and other causes, etc.)
- o I serve in the church because I feel like I should, not because I really want to

PHYSICAL:
- o I wake up after 7-9 hours of sleep still tired
- o I rarely exercise
- o I do not take a day of Sabbath on a regular basis
- o I have one or more of these issues on a regular basis: headaches, digestion issues, diarrhea, or constipation

- I tend to reach for junk food instead of eating a healthy diet
- I tend to drink soda, coffee, or tea more often than I do water
- I overeat or eat for comfort or the reward of pleasure
- My muscles are tight in my neck, shoulders or jaw

EMOTIONAL:
- I spend a considerable amount of time focusing on my outward appearance
- One of these substances (food, drug type substances, caffeine, alcohol) or processes (television, computer, people, porn) help me cope or feel better when I am stressed or lonely
- Negative thinking has almost become a habit for me
- Negative self-talk (thinking or speaking negative words about myself) has become a frequent practice for me
- I use cutting sarcasm as humor
- I spend more time on the internet or watching television than relating to God
- I've been procrastinating quite a bit lately
- I'm feeling down, discouraged or depressed these days
- My life feels chaotic
- My nerves are on edge and I'm feeling irritable…again
- I take little time to self-reflect or journal
- I don't have anyone I can be transparent with and accountable to
- I lack a peaceful heart and spirit
- It is difficult for me to talk about my feelings with others

Make a careful observation of the statements that you have checked. Which area of your life is being neglected the most and in what way? What are you willing to do about it?

Chapter 4

Hindrances to Being Holy and Whole

Since our body, mind, and spirit function together as a whole, the balance of our body can be disturbed by many different kinds of issues. As you read the following list, you may find things that are disturbing the balance in your life. To the right of each issue, you will notice some ideas for restoring the balance in that area.

Things that may Disturb Balance	Things that may help Restore Balance
Being too busy; rushing	Re-evaluate your time commitments; Take time for silence and solitude on a daily basis[68]
Holding grudges (unforgiveness can set up a wall between you and God, as well as others)	Forgive yourself and others; Surrender your hurt to God; Repent[69]
Stress; anxiety	Talk to a friend or counselor; Learn to release your cares to God;[70] Use music as therapy;[71] Learn to trust God with your cares; Take stress inventory in Appendix D
Perfectionism; too serious	Establish a healthy view of self; Exchange lies for truth

---

[68] Ps. 46:10

[69] Ps. 51

[70] I Pet. 5:7

[71] Col. 3:16

Not enough sleep	Re-evaluate your time commitments; Take time for daily exercise to release stress and help you relax; take time for a Sabbath;[72]
Not breathing properly	Learn some breathing techniques; Take time to do some stretching and breathing exercises
Unresolved and unhealed hurts or wounds	Find healing through the use of Inner Healing prayer,[73] forgive those who've hurt you
Lies we believe	Learn to identify the lies you are believing and exchange them for God's Truth[74]
Negative attitude	Practice gratitude; Feed daily on Scripture and on thoughts that feed the mind[75]
Selfishness; self-centeredness	Learn to imitate Christ;[76] Read gospels daily; Surrender your will to God each day; Practice gratitude; move focus from problems to God your resource
Attempting to be in control	Pray the Serenity Prayer each day; Surrender control over to God; Re-evaluate your view of God and view of self

[72] Exo. 20:8

[73] Ps. 147:3

[74] Rom. 1:25

[75] Phil. 4:8

[76] Phil. 2:4-8

As you examine this list, you will notice that there are many obstacles that can keep us from growing in Christ. In addition, there are things outside us, such as neglect and abuse (spiritual, physical, and sexual) that can also be obstacles to our growth. Such things can distort our view of God and our view of who we are in Christ.

Along with this comes the struggle we encounter with our own pride, selfishness, and sinfulness. The sinfulness of Adam, which became our inheritance, disrupted God's plan of wholeness for us; yet God provided a way, through the death and sacrifice of Jesus, for our continuous restoration to his original plan. God desires that we find our way "back to Eden" and to his original plan for humankind.

Another issue that hinders our wholeness is cultural pressure. Unfortunately many Christians have "pitched their tents" too close to Sodom, just as Lot did.[77] Little by little they have bought into the values of the world, looking and acting more like the culture than like God. Our current models of discipleship rarely address a holistic approach to discipleship, embracing instead a one-sided approach or "consumer discipleship" which avoids the serious teachings of Christ.[78] As a result many Christians live at a level of immaturity in their lives.

It is alarming to realize that there is often little difference between the level of emotional and relational maturity among those inside the church and outside the church. Just look in most churches and you will find broken and failed relationships, an overabundance of addictive behaviors, a throng of lonely children and spouses, a battleground of conflict, and a lack of transparency regarding one's struggles and difficulties. Many people have been Christians for a long time, but spend little time with God and seldom incorporate spiritual disciplines and habits of the heart into their daily

---

[77] Gen. 13:12

[78] Luke 14:26-27, 33; Mark 8:34-35; John 13:34-35

schedule. They are focused on things that please themselves and fail to make a relationship with God the priority of their life.

Others may seem spiritually mature, but remain children emotionally. They demonstrate little ability to process anger, sadness or hurt. They often complain, criticize, cut themselves off from others, blame, and use sarcasm. They may be competitive, highly defensive to criticism or differences of opinion, and rarely exhibit a peaceful spirit. Still others may exhibit spiritual leadership but live on junk food, rarely exercising or taking time off from a busy schedule.

What takes place in our inner person does affect our physical health and a compromised physical condition can likewise have a negative impact on our spiritual health. It may be that an issue in one area is really pointing to an issue in another. The link between emotional, spiritual, and physical maturity is still a largely unexplored area of discipleship. As we grow in this understanding we will realize that self-care involves being a steward of the entire person and should be a commitment we make to God when we choose to be a follower of Christ.

Chapter 5

Self-Leadership

Jesus chose kenosis rather than burnout. What a seeming paradox that holiness and wholeness would come through actions such as laying aside one's equality with God, emptying one's self, voluntarily and willingly stripping one's self of privileges, humbling one's self, and exercising obedience to the point of death.[79] These choices fly against the grain of today's culture and yet surprisingly free us up to focus energy on the primary issues of life. They protect us from burnout and facilitate the process of us becoming more and more like Christ, which is where true fulfillment comes from!

Christians today are eager to learn how to use their spiritual gifts and abilities in ministry to lead others, but they fail to place the same importance on self-leadership. Self-leadership involves not only spiritual soul care, but attentiveness to our physical bodies and a balance in our emotional being. Paying attention to our own self-care involves attention to all three of these areas and may seem overwhelming at times. But if we see self-care as a journey, instead of a destination, it can help us as we balance this art of caring for ourselves.

When we see self-care as a destination, our main focus will probably be to arrive at an end, one way or the other. But in a journey we focus on the process. Sometimes we focus on one area; while other times we center on something else. But all the time we want to be aware of the bigger picture, not blinded by our need to arrive at the destination of being holy and whole. For instance, if we become too focused on a particular felt need in our lives (such as self-worth or a need to be loved or affirmed), we might tend to isolate our focus on that particular need and distort the overall picture of living in

---

[79] Phil. 2:6-8 [RSV].

23

balance. A focus that involves love for God (with all of our being), a love for ourselves (based on what God says about us), along with a healthy, caring love for others will help keep us on a balanced path toward being holy and whole.[80]

Growing *spiritually* involves things such as scripture reading, talking and listening to God, spiritual disciplines, as well as journaling and spending time on personal retreats. Busyness, frustration, and laziness can be obstacles to soul care.

Being attentive to our *physical bodies* might include things such as diet and nutrition, weight management, physical fitness, rest, and recreation. A lack of personal commitment and a failure to plan for physical wholeness, as well as, procrastination and numerous hours wasted watching television and surfing the internet may keep us from growing in physical wholeness.

Being attentive to our *emotional health* might involve being aware of our feelings and responses and then reflecting on what they are saying to us. Obstacles to emotional growth include such things as a distorted view of who we are in Christ, the belief of lies (that generally originate from childhood hurts and are a tool of the enemy), and generational sins that have been modeled and passed down to us.

Because of today's fast-paced living, we often fail to notice the warning signs that indicate we need to give personal attention to our self-care. This is risky because serious problems always begin with minor indicators. I dare say that if we ignored the shimmy of an auto wheel that was out of alignment, it would eventually result in problems with our tires, the car's steering, or eventually our suspension system.

We see that being holy and whole is not only to be perceived as growth in the physical, emotional, and spiritual areas of our being, but in the very essence of our character. God desires us to be this way, but he needs our cooperation in order for it to happen!

---

[80] Matt. 22:37

Consider praying this prayer by Robert Mulholland as we journey together in this "process of becoming holy and whole"!

Gracious and loving God,
I stand in awe of your infinite patience.
You desire my perfect wholeness.
You are deeply desirous to make me perfectly whole,
even to the extent of entering into my brokenness
and taking its death into your own being on the cross.
And yet you never violate my independence,
you never trample upon my free will,
you never usurp the integrity of my being.
You wait in infinite patience for me to open my life
to your cleansing, healing, liberating, transforming grace.
You wait for me to willingly cooperate with your purposes
for my wholeness.[81]

Your Response...

You have been invited to be formed holy and whole by the master potter. How do you want to respond to his invitation? *(Write your response in the area below.)*

---

[81] Robert Mulholland, *Invitation to a Journey* (Downers Grove, IL: InterVarsity Press, 1993), 135.

GOING DEEPER ⇩

(Feel free to use the material in the two sections of Going Deeper for more than one week of group discussion.)

Reflection Questions *(for Individuals or a Group)*

CONNECTING WITH GOD
Begin with a few slow, deep breaths. Sit in silence for several minutes, allowing your mind to quiet as you focus on God.

THINKING OUTLOUD
Take time to not only answer these questions but to ask your own questions about the primary ideas of this section.

1. Ephesians 1:4 in the Message says, "Long before he laid down earth's foundations, he had us in mind, had settled on us as the focus of his love, to be made whole and holy <u>by his love</u>."

• Becoming *whole and holy* would seem like actions that depend on discipline, on our own efforts and achievements. But in Ephesians 1:4 Paul represents them as actions of (and responses to) God's love. Which one of these have you utilized most often in the past in an effort to be holy and whole (your own efforts or God's love)? Give an example.

• When you feel important and loved by someone, how does that change your response to them and desire to please them?

2. It has been said that "wholeness is developing a balanced lifestyle that promotes health and that health is soundness in all dimensions of life."

• What are your thoughts about being healthy in *all* dimensions of life? Is it realistic and possible?

3. Can Christians live a life that is holy and whole (a counter-cultural practice) in a world that seeks to influence all of our actions and decisions of life?

4. How do we decide what is God's way and the world's way in regard to not only our spiritual health, but physical, emotional, and sexual wholeness?
5. What are some of the consequences that can occur when we live our lives without attention to all parts of ourselves – physical, emotional, and spiritual?
6. Roy Oswald says, "Total health involves embracing our brokenness. Wholeness should never be seen as perfection, but rather an acknowledgment and acceptance of weakness." (Read II Cor. 12:9)
- How do you feel about brokenness and weakness being equated with wholeness?
- How has brokenness (or trials) helped you grow in Christ? Give an example of a time when you grew through a time of trial.
7. "Personal change is not a clean, clear-cut process. Like clay whirled on a potter's wheel, God seems to offer repeated opportunities to change."
- What opportunities has God been offering you lately for change and growth?

BEING FORMED BY THE WORD
Read Jeremiah 18:1-6. Meditate silently on this passage:
- Visualize yourself as the clay in the potter's hands. What does it feel like for the potter to be making the decision on what shape you are to be? (Scary, exciting, unsure, not in control, etc.) How does it feel to be clay in his hands?
- On a scale of 1-5 (one being least; 5 being most), how motivated are you for being formed "holy and whole"?

COMMITTING TO WHOLENESS
In closing, read (silently or out loud) Mulholland's prayer that can be found at the end of this section.

May you cooperate with God's purposes for your wholeness this week!

TAKING TIME TO BE FORMED

First Day:

Take the Wholeness check-up in Part 1.
- What area of your growth (physical, emotional, or spiritual) do you focus on the most?
- Which do you neglect the most? What are some ways that you can begin growing in this area?
- What is your greatest fear in this challenge of growing "holy and whole"?

Second Day:

Read Jeremiah 18:1-12 and John 15:1-4. How have you seen the potter "forming you into another pot" (Jer. 18:4) or "pruning you" (Jn. 15:4) in the past year? How has this felt? How have you experienced personal growth and change because of this? Spend a few moments talking to God about these experiences.

Third Day:

Whether it is in church leadership, parenting, our marriage, or at our jobs, we tend to communicate what we know and focus upon what to do, but we will ultimately impart who we are.

- Write a couple sentences to answer the question, "Who am I?"
- According to your answer, are you: What you "do"? What others say about you? What you "have"? What God says about you? What do your daily actions and responses tell you about who you are?

Fourth Day:

Reread the list of things (in this chapter) that can disturb the balance in your life.

- What is one that is most obvious in your life right now? Try one of the suggestions listed.

Fifth Day:

Read through the Beatitudes (Matt 5:1-12) in several different versions of the bible. (Use an online resource like BibleGateway.com if you do not have other versions handy.)

Meditate on the Beatitude that stands out the most to you and journal these thoughts:

- What is God saying to you in this beatitude? Which beatitude stands out to you?
- How is what Jesus says different than what the world says?
- As you spend time with God, invite him to develop this quality in your life.

Bibliography

Jones, E. Stanley. *Conversion.* New York: Abingdon, 1959.

Kidd, Sue Monk. *When the Heart Waits: Spiritual Direction for Life's Sacred Questions.* New York: HarperCollins Publishers, 1990.

Mulholland, Robert. *Invitation to a Journey.* Downers Grove, IL: InterVarsity Press, 1993.

Adams, Jane. *Boundary Issues: Using Boundary Intelligence to Get the Intimacy You Want and the Independence You Need in Life, Love, and Work.* Hoboken, NJ: John Wiley & Sons, 2005.

Foster, Richard J., and James Bryan Smith. *Devotional Classics.* San Francisco: HarperCollins, 1993.

Additional Resources

Oswald, Roy M. *Clergy Self-Care: Finding a Balance for Effective Ministry.* Herndon, VA: Alban Institute, 1991.

Rima, Samuel D. *Leading from the Inside out: The Art of Self-leadership.* Grand Rapids: Baker Books, 2000.

Scazzero, Peter. *The Emotionally Healthy Church: A Strategy for Discipleship that Actually Changes Lives.* Grand Rapids: Zondervan, 2003.

Sisk, Ronald D. *The Competent Pastor: Skills and Self-Knowledge for Serving Well.* Herndon, VA: The Alban Institute, 2005.

Part II

HOLY AND WHOLE in Spirit

Physical exercise has some value, but spiritual exercise
is much more important, for it promises a reward
in both this life and the next.
-I Timothy 4:8 [NLT]

The Word of God is not received by faith if it flits
about in the top of the brain, but when it takes
root in the depth of the heart.
-John Calvin

There is only one problem on which all my existence,
my peace, and my happiness depend:
to discover myself in discovering God.
If I find Him I will find myself
and if I find my true self I will find Him.
-Thomas Merton

Spirituality is a commonly used word in our culture today. There are spiritualties of all varieties - Christian, New Age, Hindu, Buddhist, Muslim, Zen, Wicca, various Eastern meditation techniques, a greater power, an eclectic spirituality, and even pop spirituality. All of these varieties have a god that they worship. For example, when someone speaks of Muslim, their god is Allah; or Buddhist's god is Buddha. Christian spirituality associates its spirituality specifically with Jesus which clearly defines who its God is.

I have found that as long as a person talks about "god" in this culture, it is acceptable by most people, but when the God is Jesus Christ it often becomes offensive. However, from a Judeo-Christian perspective no authentic spirituality exists without a defining reference to Jesus Christ and the Scriptures.[82]

When we speak of spiritual maturity, we are referring to the process whereby a person grows into a mature relationship with Jesus Christ. To be in Christ is to enjoy a vibrant, vital, organic relationship with Him, so that His life flows into us and we share His very life. This is a relationship characterized by faith, love, worship, and obedience.

In the opening address at the First International Consultation on Discipleship, John Stott challenged the audience concerning the issue of authentic discipleship and the process of maturing in Christ. He indicated that we cannot possibly claim to be mature disciples if we are living in disbelief or disobedience. Mature disciples are so closely related to Jesus Christ that they trust His promises, obey His commands, bow before Him worshiping Him, and acknowledge Him as Lord.

Where then shall we find the authentic Jesus so that we may grow in our understanding of Him and in our relationship with Him? The answer, of course, is in the Scriptures. Scripture is God's portrait of His Son, painted by the Holy Spirit. Jesus himself reminded Cleopas and his companion that the Scriptures bear witness concerning himself.[83]

---

[82] Jn. 10:7-9; Acts 4:10-12

[83] Luke 24:27

Chapter 6

Theology of Spirituality and Formation

Christian spirituality must be seen as a process not an activity. Robert Mulholland views it as a journey, not a destination. He refers to it as a "pilgrimage of deepening responsiveness to God's control of our life and being".[84] But for some, Christian spirituality is seen as a static experience, rather than a vibrant and ever-developing growth toward wholeness. From a static viewpoint spirituality belongs to us personally and becomes a way of gaining information and techniques that can help us acquire what *we* want. This allows us to stay in control of our relationship with God, instead of God being in control of our lives.

However, Scripture is not merely information; it is living and active, judging the thoughts and attitudes of our hearts.[85] It is meant to challenge us and transform us and bring us to a place where we become "less" and Christ becomes "more".[86] "Don't be selfish", Paul says…Don't look out only for your own interests",[87] but follow the example of Christ who gave up his privileges in order to be obedient to God.[88]

When spirituality is viewed this way, then all of life is seen as spiritual formation. It becomes a day-by-day continuous experience that is an "intentional and continual

---

[84] Robert Mulholland, *Invitation to a Journey* (Downers Grove, IL: InterVarsity Press, 1993), 12.

[85] Heb. 4:12

[86] Jn. 3:30

[87] Phil. 2:2-3

[88] Phil. 2:7-8 [NLT].

commitment toward wholeness". [89] However, this unhurried, sometimes difficult, process goes against the grain of our instant-gratification culture who wants to acquire things right now.

Walter Principe defines Christian spirituality as "those aspects of a person's…faith or commitment that concern his or her striving… for an ever more intense union with the *Father* through *Jesus Christ* by living in the *Spirit*." [90] This definition allows us to see our spiritual relationship in a more holistic manner, encouraging relational growth with a Trinitarian God - the Father, the Son, and the Holy Spirit. This discourages us from isolating our spiritual focus to Jesus only, God only, or Spirit only, which can limit opportunity for spiritual growth. This helps us embrace the love of the Father, the grace that comes through Jesus, and the fellowship of the Holy Spirit. [91]

Spirituality not only involves energy directed toward the triune God, but also energy directed toward people. Both movements must be plainly present in a complete spiritual life.

> The first movement [toward God] embraces the whole range of spiritual communion between the soul and God…In the second [toward people] we return, with the added peace and energy thus gained, to the natural world; there to do spiritual work for and with God for others.…Now both these movements are of course necessary in all Christians; but the point is that the second will only be well done where the *first has the central place*. The deepening of the soul's unseen attachments *must precede* the outward swing toward

---

[89] Ibid.

[90] Walter Principe, *Exploring Christian Spirituality,* ed. Kenneth J. Collins (Grand Rapids, MI: Baker Books, 2000), 51.

[91] II Cor. 13:14

the world in order to safeguard it.[92]

It is clear to see that without a continuing vital relationship with God, a person will not have a healthy, balanced relationship with others.

The most ancient term used for the study of a relationship with God was asceticism, which meant any kind of exercise or training to make progress in one's life in the Spirit. The ascetical way consisted of things such as, Biblical reading and the disciplining of one's self, even to the extreme of mortification and purgation.

Mystical was another term utilized for describing one's relationship with God, designating the experience of God as transcendental and incomprehensible, an experience that could not be achieved by one's own efforts or intellectual activity but a gift from God. The ascetical way came to be associated with the ordinary state of Christians, while the mystical was considered extraordinary, resulting in a dispute concerning the use of these terms. It was finally decided to adopt a term that didn't create opposition between the two. The French word, *spiritualité,* was deemed the most suitable to designate the spiritual life in all its phases. Hence, the word spirituality began to be associated with one's relationship with God, while spiritual theology became known as the systematic study of Christian perfection and the spiritual life.

The struggle between the ascetic and the mystical also included a tension between the two sources of spiritual growth: data (cognitive knowledge including discipline) and personal experience (relationship with God). It was found that the spiritual life actually encompassed both of these elements, making it a connection with the mind and the heart. Jesus reminds us that loving God involves the heart, the soul, and

---

[92] Evelyn Underhill, *Concerning the Inner Life: Selected Writings of Evelyn Underhill* (Nashville: Upper Room Books, 1926), 14-15 [italics added].

the mind.[93] This ensures that we will experience God on various levels, strengthening our relationship with him, safeguarding a possible disconnect that can set us up for potential problems in morality, burnout, and addictive behavior.

Today, with all the emphasis on knowledge and service (ascetic), Christians are "starved for mystery, to know this God...and to experience reverence in his presence. We are starved for intimacy, to see and feel and know God in the very cells of our being...to know God beyond what we can do for him." [94]

---

[93]Matt. 22:37; Mark 12:30; Luke 10:27

[94] Ruth Haley Barton, Invitation *to Solitude and Silence* (Downers Grove, IL: InterVarsity Press, 2004), 21.

Chapter 7

Healthy View of God and Self

*Somehow we never see God in failure, but only
in success and happiness - a strange attitude for
people who have the cross at the center of their faith.*
Cheryl Forbes

View of God

Throughout the ages humankind has adopted differing opinions concerning their view about God, such as theism, deism, atheism, agnosticism, pantheism, panentheism, creationism, and traducianism. Along with these different opinions came distortions that resulted from cult-type leaders, misinformed teaching and modeling, or lack of intentional teaching, which often resulted in ambiguity.

The way we view God and ourselves is a fundamental issue of life because all things flow from our belief about God and ourselves. These viewpoints affect everything about us – our responses, reactions, what we believe, what we say, how we act and react, how we relate to family and friends, how we parent, and how we minister.

Our view of God and self is usually developed early in life. We receive clues about how to view God from parents, pastors, Sunday school teachers, family members, our church, other authority figures, peers, culture, and media. It is important that our view of God line up with the true character of God as in the Bible because it will affect a number of things: 1) how we respond and relate to God, b) how we believe God thinks about us, which affects how we think and feel about ourselves, c) how we relate to others, and d) the position we maintain concerning moral attitudes and values.

Early in life I developed a faulty view of God. I was afraid to get too close to him for fear that I might not please him or he might reject me as others had. I also felt disappointed with him because I thought he hadn't been there for me in some of the hurtful times of my life. So how could I trust that he would really do what was best for me? It became difficult for me to grow and mature in Christ because I was encumbered by these flawed beliefs.

The fact that view of God does affect how we react and how we tend to position ourselves on moral values was substantiated by a U.S. survey conducted by Gallup on September 12, 2006. NewsMax.com provided the results of this report that surveyed more than 1,700 Americans. It asked 77 questions and offered nearly 400 answer choices. From these answers, the researchers classified view of God in four categories: the Authoritarian God, the Critical God, the Benevolent God, and the Distant God.

The Authoritarian God (31.4% of Americans overall) was based on a God who is engaged in everyone's life and worldly affairs, but is angry at humanity's sins. The Benevolent God (23% of Americans overall) was one who was seen primarily as a loving and forgiving Creator, but who also set absolute standards for mankind. The Distant God (24.4% of Americans overall) was seen as a cosmic force that launched the universe, then left it on its own. The Critical God (16% of Americans overall) was a God who kept a judgmental eye on humankind, but didn't intervene in humanity's events.

The largest percentage of people with the Authoritarian God viewpoint (43.5%) lived in the South, while the Benevolent view was most common (28.8%) in the Midwest. The Critical God was most prevalent (21.2%) in the East, while the Distant God was favored most (30.3%) in the West. This seems to indicate that people are influenced by others around them - possibly their family, their church or the long-established values of a particular area or region of the country.

An interesting detail emerged as the analysts reported that more than 80% of those who favored the Authoritarian God

38

said that gay marriage is always wrong, and 74.5% of Authoritarian responders believed the federal government should advocate Christian values. This seems to indicate that the stand these Authoritarians took on gay marriage may have been affected by their view of God, a view that was based on a God who is angry at humanity's sins. If this is true, we can see what an influence our view of God can have on our beliefs, thoughts, and reactions!

All of us have received messages concerning God throughout our lifetime, but some of these may not fit into the same view about God, resulting in mixed messages about God. As you evaluate your view of God, based on the following three perspectives, assess whether your beliefs represent mainly one viewpoint or a mixture of several.

The first viewpoint can be described as prescriptive. The prescriptive view is usually founded on long standing customs with very little room for differences. It reduces beliefs to explicit rules or codes as seen in the life of the Pharisees in the New Testament. It tends to be authoritarian, regimented, perfectionistic, and legalistic.

A person with a prescriptive view of God may tend to be afraid of God, feel he is unapproachable, and avoid his presence. The reason being is that he is viewed as an angry judge and one who expects them to be perfect. As can be imagined, this view results in a one way relationship with God based on the ascetical way (rules and discipline) and in all probability includes little of the mystical (experiential) because we tend to avoid relationships that are based on fear and perfectionism. If you are transitioning from this viewpoint to a healthier one, you may still retain a few of these perspectives or feelings. Remember, however, growth is a journey and process, not a destination. Be patient with yourself as you grow on this journey.

A second viewpoint can be described as permissive. This viewpoint can be characterized as laissez-faire, undisciplined, noncommittal, pro-normless, broad-minded, and passive. When a person adopts a permissive view of God they rarely approach God, do not feel close to him, and lack proper fear and respect for him. They feel God is lenient and too kind to punish them. They believe there are very few guidelines and norms in which to govern life. This view tends to be a relativistic perspective and is found not only in our culture today among non-Christians, but in an increasing number of Christians.

A third viewpoint is considered the most accurate view of God – the principial. This view can be seen as flexible, balanced, open, collaborative, charitable, and responsible. Principles are sufficiently abstract so that their application to a wide range of conduct is feasible without violation of the principle. From this point of view values are unalterable but methods can change, allowing for flexibility over time and space. A person with a principial view of God has a healthy fear of God, finds him approachable, is comfortable in his presence, and interacts with him out of a relationship of grace.

Pause a moment and reflect on what God's voice sounds like to you. Is it harsh and condemning or loving and grace-based? Is it angry and critical or caring and accepting? Is it demeaning and hurtful or affirming and kind? Is it afar off and silent or close and present? Is it demanding and perfectionistic or fair and forgiving? Paying attention to how his voice sounds to you will help you in determining your view of God.

Our growth toward a more accurate view of God will involve not only a "head" knowledge of who God is but a "heart" knowing. According to Scripture God is: immutable,[95] infinite,[96] everlasting,[97] omniscient,[98] omnipotent,[99]

---

[95] Mal. 3:6

[96] Ps. 147:5

[97] Ps. 90:2

[98] I Sam. 2:3 [KJV].

[99] Rev. 19:6 [AV].

transcendent,[100] faithful,[101] good,[102] just,[103] omnipresent,[104] merciful,[105] gracious,[106] loving,[107] holy,[108] and sovereign.[109] Reading and rereading who God is according to Scripture will help us to know intellectually these truths. But heart knowledge will only come as we experience these qualities of God personally and open our heart to a relationship with him by spending time with him.

In a book called *The Shack* the main character, Mackenzie, is trying to make sense of a tragedy in his life. Unfortunately he is basing his understanding on the tiny picture of reality that he is able to see at the moment. So God says to him,

The real underlying flaw in your life, Mackenzie, is that you don't think that I am good. If you knew I was good and that everything – the means, the ends, and all the processes of individual lives – is all covered by my goodness, then while you might not always understand what I am doing, you would trust me. But you don't...Mackenzie, you cannot produce trust just like you

---

[100] Ps. 57:5

[101] Lam. 3:23

[102] Ps. 27:13

[103] II Thess. 1:6

[104] Ps. 119:151

[105] Dan. 9:9

[106] II Chron. 30:9

[107] Ps. 36:7

[108] Ps. 99:2; Isa. 6:3

[109] Isa. 40:10

cannot 'do' humility. It either is or is not. Trust is the fruit of a relationship in which you know you are loved. Because you do not know that I love you, you cannot trust me.[110]

If our view of God has been skewed through painful experiences, through being injured by an authority figure, or by having experienced spiritual abuse sometime in our life, we will need to address those wounds in order for us to feel safe moving close to God. A good godly counselor or spiritual director can be a great resource in dealing with the obstacles that have closed down our heart to God.

It seems acceptable for us to focus on knowing God, but a focus on knowing our self often seems unspiritual. However, knowing God and knowing our self are interconnected and develop interactively.[111] John Calvin said, "There is no deep knowing of God without a deep knowing of self and no deep knowing of self without a deep knowing of God."[112] "People who have never developed a deep personal knowing of God...will be unable to know themselves, as God is the only context in which their being makes sense."[113]

The mental picture we have of our self, often referred to as self-image or self-identity is what could be called our view of self. It is core to our being and affects the way we act and react in life. It can be affected, not only by our view of God, but also by people's words and actions, how we think

---

[110] William P. Young, *The Shack* (Los Angeles: Windblown Media, 2007), 126.

[111] David G. Benner, *The Gift of Being Yourself: The Sacred Call to Self-Discovery* (Downers Grove, IL: InterVarsity Press, 2004).

[112] John Calvin, *Institutes of the Christian Religion,* 1536 ed., trans Ford Lewis Battles (Grand Rapids, MI: Eerdmans, 1995), 15.

[113] David G. Benner, *The Gift of Being Yourself: The Sacred Call to Self-Discovery* (Downers Grove, IL: InterVarsity Press, 2004), 25-26.

others want us to be, our outward appearance, our status and achievements, hurtful experiences in life, or the lies we believe that are distorted by the deception of Satan.

There are three basic ways to see one's self: 1) the way we think we are (mirrored, perceived self), 2) the way others think we are (masked, public self or false self), or 3) the way we really are (core, private self).[114] These three can vary significantly or be fairly consistent with each other. In a healthy self these three overlap, so that the way we act in public is consistent with how we act in private, and the way we see ourselves is the way we really are. However, we sometimes become what Tom Hanks in *You've Got Mail* called, "the worst possible version of ourselves" or sometimes called our false self.

Here are some hints in helping you to recognize your false self: defensiveness, touchiness, pettiness, a need to be important (we bristle when not taken seriously), and the pattern of our compulsions. Our compulsions represent the excessive attachments we have grabbed on to in order to hide behind; their basic function is to help us preserve our false self.

We can find many ways of measuring who we are and our worth, but the only true measure of who we are is based on what God thinks of us. So how do we find our true self? "We do not find our true self by seeking it. Rather, we find it by seeking God. For… in finding God, we find our truest and deepest self."[115]

God has communicated through the Scriptures who you really are: You are a child of God;[116] you are chosen of

---

[114] The DISC Personality Profile will assess your scores in all three areas. See Appendix B for more information on the DISC profile.

[115] David G. Benner, *The Gift of Being Yourself: The Sacred Call to Self-Discovery* (Downers Grove, IL: InterVarsity Press, 2004), 91.

[116] Jn. 1:12

God;[117] holy and dearly loved;[118] you are redeemed and forgiven of all your sins;[119] you are a joint heir with Christ, sharing in His inheritance;[120] you are a new creation;[121] you are more than a conqueror through Him who loves you;[122] you are complete through your union with Christ.[123]

Listen to how much God loves you:

- I have loved you with an everlasting love. With unfailing love I have drawn you to myself.[124]
- Though the mountains are shaken and the hills be removed, yet my unfailing love for you will not be shaken.[125]
- Nothing will be able to separate you from the love of God that is in Christ Jesus your Lord.[126]
- Can a mother forget her nursing child? Can she feel no love for a child she has borne?   But even if that were possible, I would not forget you! See, I have written your name on my hand.[127]

---

[117] Eph. 1:11

[118] Col. 3:12, I Thess. 1:4

[119] Col. 1:14

[120] Rom. 8:17

[121] II Cor. 5:17

[122] Rom. 8:37

[123] Col. 2:10 [NLT].

[124] Jer. 31:3-4

[125] Isa. 54:10-11

[126] Rom. 8:39

[127] Isa. 49:15-16

44

- I created your inmost being; I knit you together in your mother's womb. You are fearfully and wonderfully made.[128]
- I take great delight in you, I will quiet you with my love, and will rejoice over you with singing.[129]
- Do not be afraid, for I have ransomed you. I have called you by name; you are mine…You are precious to me. I love you.[130]
- This is how I showed my love for you: I sent my one and only Son into the world that you might live through Him.[131]
- You are my masterpiece, created anew in Christ Jesus.[132]
- I know the plans I have for you…plans to prosper you and not to harm you, plans to give you hope and a future.[133]

It may be hard to imagine but God's love has nothing to do with our behavior. God's "divine love is absolutely unconditional, unlimited and, unimaginably extravagant."[134]

Jesus talked about loving God and loving others when He wrapped up the commandments into these simple words, "Love the Lord your God with all your heart and with all your soul and with all your mind. This is the first and greatest commandment. And the second is like it: Love your neighbor as yourself."[135] Loving *God* completely is the key to loving

---

[128] Ps. 139:13-14

[129] Zep. 3:17

[130] Isa. 43:1-5

[131] I Jn. 4:9

[132] Eph. 2:10 [NLT].

[133] Jer. 29:11

[134] David Benner, *The Gift of Being Yourself: The Sacred Call to Self-Discovery* (Downers Grove, IL: InterVarsity Press, 2004), 49.

[135] Matt. 22:37

self correctly (seeing ourselves as God sees us), and this in turn is the key to loving *others* compassionately.

Chapter 8

Spirituality Embraces Body, Soul and Spirit

Benner describes the essence of spirituality in a number of ways:[136] as a commitment,[137] as obedience to God,[138] an identity,[139] a call to follow Jesus,[140] a relationship with God,[141] and the response of spirit to Spirit.[142] These descriptions are meant to embrace an experience with God not only in spirit, but in body, and in soul. Trying to define these three entities however can be difficult, for they are not totally separate, but work in collaboration with one another. A similar challenge occurs when we try to understand the trinity – one God with three beings - the Father, the Son, and the Spirit.

Paul makes reference to the three basic entities of man when he says, "May God himself, the God of peace, sanctify you through and through. May your whole *spirit, soul, and body* be kept blameless at the coming of our Lord Jesus Christ."[143] Paul is telling us in this verse that God wants to make us holy and whole (sanctify us) in all three entities - spirit, soul and body - in preparation for the final coming of Jesus. However, trying to define these three entities can be

---

[136] Ibid.

[137] I Sam. 7:3; Josh. 24:14-15

[138] II Jn. 1:6

[139] I Pet. 2:9, Col. 3:12

[140] Matt. 16:24, Luke 5:32

[141] Rom. 8:15-17

[142] John 3:5-6; Rom. 8:5

[143] I Thess. 5:23 [italics added].

difficult, for they are not totally separate but work in collaboration with one another. A similar challenge occurs when we try to understand the trinity – one God with three beings - the Father, the Son, and the Spirit.

Even though holistic in nature, distinctions can be noted regarding the spirit, soul, and body. The spirit is the vital principle - the inner, effective, energizing and divine principle of life. It represents the part of us created in the image of God so that we can know God and enjoy His fellowship. It is our new nature that is born of the *Spirit.*[144] The same Greek word, *pneuma,* used for the human spirit is also used for the Spirit of God.

While in the Garden of Gethsemane Jesus speaks these words to his disciples, "The *spirit* (pneuma) is willing, but the body is weak."[145] In contrast we are called to live in accordance with the *Spirit* (pneuma) and have our minds on what the *Spirit* desires.[146] Paul reminds us "he who unites himself with the Lord is one with him in *spirit* (pneuma)."[147] In Hebrews we learn that the "word of God is living and active... it penetrates even to dividing soul and *spirit*,"[148] the two invisible, nonmaterial parts of man.

The soul is referred to in this way, "And the LORD God formed man of the dust of the ground, and breathed into his nostrils the breath of life; and man became a living soul."[149] The soul is the immaterial, invisible part of man;[150] the seat of

---

[144] Jn. 3:6

[145] Matt. 26:41 [italics added].

[146] Rom. 8:5

[147] I Cor. 6:17

[148] Heb. 4:12 [italics added].

[149] Gen. 2:7 [KVJ].

[150] Matt. 10:28

personality;[151] the part of man that perceives, reflects, feels, desires;[152] the seat of will and purpose;[153] the seat of appetite.[154] When Hebrew 4:12 speaks of the word of God dividing soul and spirit, it reminds us of the "extreme difficulty of distinguishing between the soul and the spirit, alike in their nature and in their activities. Generally speaking the spirit is the higher, the soul the lower element."[155]

The body contains physical organs and is the earthly house or tent we live in.[156] It is the part of our being from which come our physical needs and drives. God has designed the body with normal appetites that can be met in life-sustaining ways or can be met in ways that are destructive.

Vine offers the following distinctions for the spirit, soul, and body. "The spirit may be recognized as the life principle bestowed on man by God; the soul as the resulting life constituted in the individual; the body being the material organism animated by soul and spirit."[157]

As previously mentioned, these parts (body, soul and spirit) work together in a combined effort. When the body and soul are integrated together, the body can become the expression of the soul. For example, the body, in the form of the voice, expresses our inner emotions and thoughts in the

---

[151] Luke 9:24, Matt. 8:36

[152] Matt. 11:29, Luke 1:46

[153] Acts 4:32, Matt. 22:37

[154]Rev. 18:14, Ps. 107:9

[155] W.E. Vine, *Expository Dictionary of New Testament Words* (Grand Rapids, MI: Zondervan, 1982), 54.

[156] II Cor. 5:1

[157] W.E. Vine, *Expository Dictionary of New Testament Words* (Grand Rapids, MI: Zondervan, 1982), 54.

form of prayer to God. The hands, raised in praise, and the knees, bowed in humble adoration, express the passion of our soul. The body, though, will return to the earth from which it came; the soul will live on forever.

Spirit

Our whole Being

Soul   Body

Take a look at the triangle shown above and notice that if the triangle is sitting on its base, one point is up. The spirit, the divine principle, is intended to be in that upper or dominant position. But what do you suppose will happen if you allow your soul to be in that upward, authoritative position instead? You will be ruled by your feelings, thoughts, or personality type; but they are not meant to control you. Correspondingly, if your body is in the upward position and ruling, your fleshly appetites and physical drives and habits take over and become your master. The element meant to be in the upward position in order to safeguard our walk with God is the spirit. It is with the *spirit* that we relate to and connect with God; it is in accord with His *Spirit* that we are able to trust and believe.

At the time of their deaths, both Jesus and Stephen refers to their spirit *(pneuma)* being received,[158] which represents their connection with God. In John 4:24 we are reminded that

---

[158] Luke 23:46, Acts 7:59

"God is spirit *(pneuma)* and his worshipers must worship in spirit *(pneuma)* and truth. The use of the same Greek word in both instances reinforces the belief that the way we connect with God's spirit *(pneuma)* is through the spirit *(pneuma)*. Paul reminds us that "Since we live by the Spirit, let us keep in step with the Spirit,"[159] showing the importance of staying in touch with God's spirit in order to live God-focused lives.

Even though we experience God in all three, the body, the soul, and the spirit, we must live in the Spirit or we will not please God.[160] Instead, we will be ruled by sinful desires[161] or physical drives or feelings. "For the sinful nature desires what is contrary to the Spirit….They are in conflict with each other, so that (we) do not do what (we) want."[162] "Those who live according to the sinful nature have their minds set on what that nature desires; but those who live in accordance with the Spirit have their minds set on what the Spirit desires."[163]

What are some things that can hinder the spirit from being in the upward prominent position? The first thing is sin in our lives. After David had sinned by his adulterous relationship with Bathsheba, he pleaded with God to create in him a pure heart and renew a steadfast spirit *(pneuma)* within him.[164]

Besides sin, pride can get in the way of the spirit being in the prominent position. We are told in the scriptures that "pride goes before destruction, a haughty spirit before a fall"[165] and that "a man's pride brings him low, but a man of

---

[159] Gal. 5:25

[160] Rom. 8:8

[161] Gal. 5:16

[162] Gal. 5:17

[163] Rom. 8:5

[164] Ps. 51:10

[165] Prov. 16:18

51

lowly *spirit* gains honor".[166] Our strong will of independence, pride, and stubbornness can hinder us from surrendering to God. Instead, God is calling us to an attitude of trust, submission, and humility which can help keep the spirit in the dominant position[167].

Friendship with the world will also affect the spirit from being in the upward position. "Friendship with the world is hatred toward God…Anyone who chooses to be a friend of the world becomes an enemy of God."[168] The Amplified bible gives this piercing description of being a friend of the world, "You [are like] unfaithful wives [having illicit love affairs with the world and breaking your marriage vow to God]."[169] When we "buy into" the values of the culture, we sell out to the world and sacrifice the spirit being in the dominant position in our lives.[170] We are choosing to allow the world more influence in our life than God, which will in turn affect our relationship with Christ.

Attempting to meet our own physical needs, drives, and appetites with something other than God can also be a hindrance to the spirit being in the prominent position. This places the body in the prominent position and weakens the Spirit's control in our lives. The Scriptures remind us that "the spirit is willing, but the body is weak."[171] That's because flesh gives birth to flesh but the "Spirit gives birth to spirit."[172] You will become one with whatever you put in the place of

---

[166] Prov. 29:23

[167] Matt. 5:3; James 4:6-8; I Pet. 5:5-6

[168] Jas. 4:4

[169] Jas. 4:4 [AMP].

[170] Gen. 19:25-26; I Pet.2:11-12; I John 2:15-17

[171] Matt. 26:41

[172] Jn. 3:6

prominence in your life. Paul reminds us of this when he poses the question, "Do you not know that he who unites himself with a prostitute is one with her in *body*? ...But he who unites himself with the Lord is one with him in *spirit*."[173]

Additional things that can hinder the spirit from being in the prominent position are fear, lack of trust in God, an incorrect view of God or self, and unforgiveness. In reality anything that creates a barrier between us and God can cause us to close down our heart and mind and hinder our growth in spiritual wholeness.

Peter Scazzero[174] offers a list of ten top symptoms that indicate if someone has a bad case of emotionally unhealthy spirituality:

1. Using God to run from God (we create a great deal of '*God-activity*' and ignore a relationship with God and areas in our life God wants to change)
2. Ignoring the emotions of anger, sadness, and fear
3. Dying to the wrong things (we are not called by God to die to the 'good' parts of who we are or to the healthy desires of life, but to the false constructs we have accumulated that hinder our true selves from emerging)
4. Denying the past's impact on the present
5. Dividing our lives into "secular" and "sacred" compartments (compartmentalizing God to mainly 'Christian activities')
6. "Doing for God" instead of "being with God"
7. Spiritualizing away conflict (smoothing over disagreements to keep unity and peace)
8. Covering over brokenness, weakness, and failure (presenting an image of ourselves as together in front of others)
9. Living without limits and boundaries
10. Judging other people's spiritual journey

---

[173] I Cor. 6:16-17 [italics added].

[174] Peter Scazzero, Emotionally *Healthy Spirituality* (Nashville, TN: Thomas Nelson, 2006).

Since it is clear that the spirit should be placed in the upward, ruling position, how can it be maintained in that place? First, it requires the indwelling of the Holy Spirit in our lives. On the day of Pentecost, the disciples in the upper room were filled with the Spirit.[175] This happened as they were willing and open to receive the Spirit's presence and influence in their lives. Later in the NT we find others repenting, being baptized and also being filled with the Spirit.[176] We must remember, however, that the infilling is the work of the Spirit, not something we can do ourselves. We must be willing, but it is God who puts "his Spirit in our hearts as a deposit, guaranteeing what is to come."[177] It is *our* willingness, but *God's* action.

Second, the spirit can be maintained in the upward position as we repeatedly yield to the Holy Spirit's control in our lives. This involves not only an acceptance of the Spirit in our lives, but the actions of denying ourselves and taking up our own cross,[178] crucifying our old self,[179] losing our life for Christ's sake,[180] making Christ the priority of our lives,[181] giving up everything,[182] obeying what Christ commands,[183] along with a continuous surrendering to the Spirit. These

---

[175] Acts 2:4

[176] Acts 2:38; 8:14-17; 9:17-18

[177] II Cor. 1:22

[178] Luke 9:23

[179] Rom. 6:6, Gal. 2:20

[180] Matt. 10:39

[181] Luke 14:26-27, 33

[182] Luke 14:33

[183] Jn. 14:15, 23-24, 15:10

54

instructions come from the words of Jesus and will cost us everything. But they will offer us life abundant, "holding promise for both the present life and the life to come."[184]

Third, our connection with the Spirit can be strengthened as we allow God to transform us through trials. Trials can help break a stubborn spirit, which may be selfish and wanting to be in control. Through his trials Job's spirit was broken.[185] Living through brokenness is never easy, but the Psalmist reminds us that the Lord is close (connected) to the brokenhearted and saves those who are crushed in spirit.[186] God lives with those who are contrite and lowly in spirit.[187] Suffering can bring us closer to God and gives us the opportunity to be more dependent on him.

In addition, if you will take a fearless inventory of your life, based on the principles of spiritual, emotional, and spiritual wholeness and allow God to transform you one day at a time, you will find fewer barriers to keeping the spirit - in connection with God's Spirit - in the prominent position. It will be important for you to regularly examine your life, observing which element is in the upward, authoritative position - the body, the soul, or the spirit. As you continue to surrender to the Lord, you are placing the spirit in the upward, dominant position, allowing the Spirit to form and transform your life.

---

[184] I Tim. 4:8

[185] Job 17:1

[186] Ps. 34:18

[187] Isa. 57:15

Chapter 9

Spiritual Disciplines

It has been found that the cultivation of spiritual disciplines can also help our spirit stay in the dominate position. They can be described as "practices, habits, and ways of seeing and knowing that make us both attentive and responsive to the presence of God's living Spirit."[188] They can be useful in the process of spiritual growth because they help connect us most directly with God's transforming love. In connection with God spiritual disciplines can help strengthen and transform our character, mind and behavior.[189]

Spiritual disciplines are the God-ordained means to help us grow in godly ways.[190] They offer us a way to place ourselves before God as "a living sacrifice."[191] They develop habits of the heart that work indirectly to transform us. They are the product of a synergy between divine and human initiative; they are both active and passive, both initiatory and receptive.

However, we must remember that spiritual disciplines have no value in and of themselves. If they become self-indulgent, they allow us to feel prideful in our accomplishment. They can become law- driven, without real meaning.

At one time in my life I measured spiritual life in superficial ways: reading a certain number of Bible verses daily, serving actively in the church, and an avoidance of the don'ts that certain church people had decided were important.

---

[188] Stanley Saunders, "Learning Christ," *Interpretation* 56, no.2 (April 2002): 156.

[189] Rom. 12:2, Heb. 5:14, Heb. 12:11

[190] I Tim. 4:7

[191] Rom. 12:1

I had also been influenced by secular culture and the religious subculture and had bought into the idea that productivity and doing was better than being. Instead of freeing me to be in relationship with God, they enveloped me in a busyness that distracted me from him.

E Stanley Jones maintains that "You cannot attain salvation by disciplines – it is the gift of God. But you cannot retain it (salvation) without disciplines. If you try to attain salvation by disciplines you will be trying to discipline an unsurrendered self."[192] Spiritual disciplines as external practices must reflect and reinforce internal aspirations and must focus more on the process of inner transformation than on outward routines. They must always be seen in the context of an intimate, personal walk with Christ, assisting in the greater purpose of knowing and serving God. And it is always easier "do" spiritual practices than to follow the difficult road of surrendering one's self to "becoming" Christ-like through the use of the practices.[193] This was true for the Pharisees and many of the other followers of Jesus Christ during his life here on earth.[194]

Countless books have been written on the topic of spiritual formation and the spiritual disciplines. However, Richard Foster is concerned that too much of the topic has become faddish and too formulaic and simply "takes up the all too familiar recipe of consumer-Christianity-without-discipleship."[195]

---

[192] E. Stanley Jones, *Conversion* (Nashville: Abingdon Press, 1959), 210.

[193] Matt. 23:25-28

[194] Matt. 23:25-28; John 6:66

[195] Richard Foster, *Spiritual Formation: A Pastoral Letter* (Englewood, CO: Renovare, 2004), http://www.theooze.com/articles/article.cfm?id=744 (accessed April 28, 2006).

Dallas Willard, author of *The Spirit of the Disciplines,* uses two categories to describe the spiritual disciplines – the disciplines of abstinence (denying one's self) and the disciplines of engagement (entering into). These two actions can be compared in a sense to our physical breathing - breathing in and breathing out, both being essential to our physical existence. One without the other creates a sense of imbalance in our spiritual lives. Disciplines of abstinence, such as silence, solitude, fasting, simplicity, and sacrifice create the inward movement of our soul.

Whereas, disciplines of engagement, such as study, prayer, meditation, confession, submission, service, worship, celebration, and guidance, develop the outward movement of our soul. We will take a closer look at the spiritual disciplines of solitude, silence, simplicity, and fasting, disciplines of abstinence since these seem particularly challenging to leaders and laypersons alike.[196]

Henri Nouwen writes these words to a personal friend, "As I grow older, I discover more and more that the greatest gift I have to offer is my own joy of living, my own inner peace, my own silence and solitude, my own sense of well-being."[197] This is why Satan would prefer for us to get caught up in hurry, noise, and crowds. When we rush, stay continually busy, live constantly with noise around us, and fail to spend time alone with God, we are kept from experiencing the peace and joy God has for us. And when we are distracted by these things, we are unable to hear the gentle whisper of God's voice."[198]

---

[196] For further information on the other disciplines, try reading the books by Foster, Whitney or Willard found in the additional resource section at the end of this chapter.

[197] Henri Nouwen, *Life of the Beloved: Spiritual Living in a Secular World* (New York: Crossroad Publishing Company, 1992), 90.

[198] I Kings 19:11-13

Christians tend to be so busy "doing" God's work that they fail to take the time to fill their own souls. "Sometimes we are in such a hurry to transmit that we forget our primary duty is to receive; and that God's self-imparting through us, will be in direct proportion to our adoring love and humble receptiveness. Only when our souls are filled to the brim, can we presume to offer spiritual gifts to others."[199]

Proverbs reminds us, "Above all else, guard your heart for it is the wellspring of life."[200] The English Standard version states that from the heart flows the "springs of life". Why should we guard our heart? We guard it because that is where our actions flow from and where life starts! This passage doesn't say to guard your heart because it is evil, but because it is a treasure. What are you doing today to care for your heart? Do you know that everything in your life depends on it?

How do we care for our hearts? We take time to be with God and allow him to fill our hearts and very being. This will mean time in silence and solitude, reading his words, listening and conversing back and forth with him. Jesus knew this; he refused to live by other people's expectations when they chased after him for his ministry.[201] He took time with God and it filled him so that he could give back to others.

You also will need to take time away from the "crowds" and the hurry, to fill yourself with God and allow your soul to catch up with your body. You will also need to take some downtime for "soul refreshment" and time to nurture yourself in God's nature in order to regain a peacefulness of heart and soul. Find out what nurtures and fills you. If then you are wise, you will show yourself rather as a reservoir, than as a canal.

---

[199] Evelyn Underhill, *The Soul's Delight: Selected Writings of Evelyn Underhill* (Nashville: Upper Room Books, 1926), 15-16.

[200] Prov. 4:23

[201] Mark 1:35-36, Luke 15-16

To be an effective spiritual leader or servant of Christ we must store up reserves within ourselves from which to minister to others. It can be compared to the difference between a canal and a reservoir. A canal releases its water as soon as it receives it and will run dry quickly after a rain fall. But a reservoir is deep and has reserves. It waits until it is full before spilling over and in that way it never suffers a loss to itself. "We are called to live in a way that we store up reserves in our hearts and *then* offer from a place of abundance."[202] Otherwise, we serve from a position of scarcity and have stored up only the bare necessities. Luke 6:45 reminds us "the good man brings good things out of the good stored up in his heart...For out of the overflow of his heart his mouth speaks".

Do you live and serve from the reservoir or the canal? It will affect all of life. Caring for our own heart is not selfish; if self- care flows out of our love and reverence for God, it will not be self-centered and egotistical but carried out for the sake of others. Will you have anything to bring to others if your heart is empty and dried up? Be reminded that how you take care of your own heart is how you will handle the heart of others.

Disciplines of Abstinence

Silence

Silence is fasting from speaking in order to hear God; it is the posture of listening. "As ministers our greatest temptation is toward too many words. They weaken our faith and make us lukewarm. But silence is a sacred discipline, a guard of the Holy Spirit."[203] Silence gives us a chance to attend and listen

---

[202] John Eldredge, *Waking the Dead* (Nashville: Thomas Nelson, 2003), 209.

[203] Henri Nouwen, *The Way of the Heart* (New York: Ballantine Books, 1981), 40.

to God in quiet, without interruption and noise. However, silence goes beyond just mere quietness.

It is the deep inner reversal of that grasping, controlling mode of being that so characterizes life in our culture...Without the practice of silence, these cultural habits will attach themselves to our spiritual disciplines...Silence is bringing ourselves to a point of relinquishing to God our control of our relationship with God...control of our own existence...Silence is the inner act of letting it go.[204]

In silence we become aware of the multiple layers of control that we exercise, our defensive postures, our attempts at justification, our indulgent habits, our manipulative practices, and the ways we use God. It is in learning to be silent that we can truly begin to practice another one of the disciplines of abstinence - solitude.

Solitude

Dallas Willard believes that solitude is the most radical of the disciplines for life in the spirit. Prison officials are aware of this and therefore use solitary confinement to break the strongest of wills. Jesus began his ministry with forty formative days of solitude. In solitude he was tempted with the urge to be relevant, spectacular, and powerful. But in that time of solitude he was able to affirm God as the "only source of his identity"[205] Solitude is difficult because it forces us to look at ourselves. So, we often choose to stay busy so that we don't

---

[204] Robert Mulholland, *Invitation to a Journey* (Downers Grove, IL: InterVarsity Press, 1993), 137.

[205] Henri Nouwen, *The Way of the Heart* (New York: Ballantine Books, 1981), 14.

have to face the many seductive visitors that pound on our door.[206]

Solitude is fasting from time with others in order to be alone with God. It is a formative place because it gives the Spirit time and space to do his work. But it is uncomfortable because all the distractions of life are left behind and we stand before God without props.

St. Anthony, the "father of monks" experienced a terrible trial during his time of solitude in the desert. "The shell of his superficial securities was cracked and the abyss of iniquity was opened to him."[207] He came out of this time victoriously, not because of his own willpower, but because of his unconditional surrender to the Lordship of Jesus Christ. He emerged from this period and spent the rest of his life in productive ministry. It is said of him, "The solitude that at first had required physical isolation had now become a quality of his heart, an inner disposition that could no longer be disturbed by those who needed his guidance. Somehow his solitude had become an infinite space into which anyone could be invited."[208]

Throughout his three years of ministry Jesus returned again and again to solitude, where the rush of attention, as well as the words of disapproval, could be put into proper perspective.

If we don't have a strong sense of who we are in Christ, we simply seem to lose our sense of self when there is no one to mirror back who we are. Without the oxygen of doing and the mirror of approval, our feelings of being real and important evaporate... (In solitude) our soul feels empty and bare. We can feel agitated, scattered and distracted. These disconcerting

---

[206] Ibid., 15.

[207] Ibid., 7.

[208] Ibid., 19.

feelings do two things for us. They reveal how much of our identity is embedded in a false sense of self. And they show us how easy it is to avoid solitude because we dislike being unproductive and unapplauded.[209]

Bonhoeffer makes a startling statement concerning solitude, "Let him who cannot be alone beware of community."[210]

> Without solitude we are dangerous in human community...because we are at the mercy of our compulsions, compelled by our inner emptiness into a self-oriented, anxious search for fullness in the next round of activities, accomplishments or relationships. When we are not finding ourselves loved by God in solitude, in the company of others we are always on the prowl for ways they can fill our emptiness. We enter life in community trying to grab and grasp from others what only God can give.[211]

Simplicity

Clutter experts maintain that we use around 20% of what we own but we maintain 100%. We have a tendency in our western culture to have an inordinate attachment to owning and having which we have grown to believe is normal. However, the well-known missionary doctor, Albert Schweitzer, stressed that if we own something we cannot give

---

[209] Adele Ahlberg Calhoun, *Spiritual Disciples Handbook: Practices that Transform us* (Downers Grove, IL: InterVarsity Press, 2005), 113.

[210] Dietrich Bonhoeffer, *Life Together* (New York: Harper, 1954), 78.

[211] Ruth Haley, *Invitation to solitude and silence* (Downers Grove, IL: InterVarsity Press, 2004), 132-133.

away, then we don't own it, it owns us. Martin Luther pointed out that if our goods were not available to the community, they were in essence already stolen goods. Jesus reminded us "Do not store up for yourselves treasures on earth...for where your treasure is, there your heart will be also" (Matt. 6:19-21).

How often do we stop to recognize that the earthly treasures we are gathering and accumulating are making their way into our hearts as well as our lives? In time they act as insulation between us and God, building a barrier that blocks off the air of God's Spirit from our lives. Practicing the spiritual discipline of simplicity can help us uncomplicate our lives so we can focus on what really matters. Letting go and loosening our connection to a cluttered and complicated life can bring freedom and along with it, generosity.

We have also bought into the principle that a good life is defined by how full, busy, and complex our lives are and that success is defined by the number of tasks we do, programs we organize, and the number of entries on our calendar. Simplicity "creates margins and spaces and openness in our lives...it offers us the leisure of tasting the present moment."[212]

Downsizing possessions, cutting back on shopping, going on a simple vacation, eating more simply, doing less, and setting priorities that flow from loving God, above everything else, are ways to practice the spiritual discipline of simplicity. However, just getting rid of some of our possessions or letting go of a few scheduled activities on our calendar will not adequately deal with this issue. We may have a time where we unclutter, but if we do not change our heart, within a short period of time we will start to gather again. That's because it is not just an issue of action or doing but an issue of the heart. We need a heart change, a change of

---

[212] Adele Ahlberg Calhoun, *Spiritual Disciples Handbook: Practices that Transform us* (Downers Grove, IL: InterVarsity Press, 2005), 75.

desire. This is where surrender and change of heart must precede the actions of obedience. Otherwise, this habit will repeat itself over and over.

Fasting

Fasting can be seen as the desire to let go of some type of appetite in order to seek God on issues of concern for others, ourselves, and the world. Adele Calhoun defines fasting as a denial of normal needs or desires in order to intentionally attend to God. "Bringing attachments and cravings to the surface opens a place for prayer. This physical awareness of emptiness is the reminder to turn to Jesus who alone can satisfy." [213] The physical awareness of emptiness reminds us to turn to Jesus who alone can satisfy the true needs of our heart and life.

Fasting has been a part of the Christian tradition for many years. Scripture offers many examples concerning the issue. People fasted at times of mourning,[214] during times of repentance,[215] and at times when they needed strength or help in persevering.[216]

However, fasting is not a way to get what you want, as seen in the example of David when he fasted for God to spare the life of Bathsheba's child.[217] Neither is it to be done for the wrong reasons, such as for appearances.[218] It is not a magical way to manipulate God, but a way to open us up to seeking

---

[213] Ibid., 218.

[214] Neh. 1:4

[215] I Sam 7:6

[216] Est. 4:16

[217] II Sam. 12:16-20

[218] Matt. 6:16

God's will. It reminds us how attached we are to food, objects, and pleasures and can help facilitate the turning of our attention back to God.

Even though fasting has normally been connected with the withdrawal from food, we can also fast from many other things: shopping, certain kinds of food (i.e. desserts, chocolate, and caffeine), media, comforts, and attachments. This act of self-denial may or may not seem like a big sacrifice, but it can bring us face-to-face with the hunger at the core of our being; it can help us recognize what controls us. "Fasting exposes how we try to keep empty hunger at bay and gain a sense of well-being by devouring creature comforts"[219] It allows us to pause and taste the difference between what truly nourishes our soul and what is simply soul junk food.

Lectio Divina

Lectio divina or "sacred reading" is a powerful way to encounter God in scripture. It includes both disciplines of abstinence (silence and contemplation) as well as disciplines of engagement (prayer and meditation). Tony Jones describes lectio divina as a process of coming before the Lord naked in order to be clothed by his Word.[220] In lectio you read the Bible as a sacred object, as a living, dynamic revelation of God to you. After a time of silence, there are four foundational steps in the practice of lectio divina – reading, meditation, prayer, and contemplation.

Here are a few helpful suggestions for lectio: Avoid using a Bible with notes or underlined passages, choose a quiet place, select a *short* text of scripture on which to meditate, and read the text slowly in order to get the most out it. Always begin lectio with a time of silence (*silencio*), opening your

---

[219] Ibid., 220.

[220] Tony Jones, *The Sacred Way* (Grand Rapids, MI: Zondervan, 2004).

heart to the presence of God. The following explanation can assist you as you encounter God through the sacred reading of his Word:

1. Silence (*silencio*). Become quiet and open your heart to the presence of God.
2. Read the Word (*lectio*). Begin reading the text *slowly* several times in order to savor what you are reading. Pay attention to the words of the text and see if a particular word or phrase stands out to you.
3. Meditate (*meditatio*). As you meditate on the passage, take time to reflect on the meaning of the text and the emotions and feelings that are arising in you. Enter into the scene in your imagination and pay attention to the senses that are evoked through the words.
4. Prayer (*oratio*). In a sense lectio is meant to be a prayer from beginning to end, but at this point allow the Scripture to lead you into a prayer response.
5. Contemplate (*contemplatio*). Take some time for a period of silence as you rest in God's presence. What is God saying to you through this text?

Prayer

We often think prayer is *only* talking to God. But prayer is really communication with God which always involves talking, listening, and even silence. Any relationship will be affected or suffer if we choose only to talk and not listen. There are many excellent books being published today on prayer and spending time with God. Some authors that I particularly enjoy are Henri Nouwen, Robert Mulholland, David Benner, and Richard Foster.

Learning to listen to God's voice is one of the most important spiritual disciplines for a believer in Christ. This can be difficult in our culture because we are surrounded by hurry, noise, and crowds. Here are some thoughts on hearing God's voice that I have found helpful:

1. *Begin by expecting to hear God's voice.* You will not hear God's voice unless you expect to. "Speak, God, I'm your servant, ready to listen."[221]
2. *Take time to sit in silence, listening to God.* If you do not take the time to really listen to a friend or spouse, you will miss what they are saying to you. The same is true with God. Try going about your day with an attitude of listening for God's voice in the daily events of the day. Tune your heart to hear and know his voice.
3. *Remember to ask God first!* When you sense a need in someone's life, ask God how he would have you pray for them. Stop and listen for what he says to you and then pray!
4. *Examples:* In Acts 8:26-29, Acts 10:19-20, and I Samuel 3:9-14 you will find some examples of others who have heard God speak. What do you notice about how God speaks?
5. *Distractions and blocked airways.* Sometimes we fail to hear God's voice because Satan is throwing distractions in our way or blocking the airways. Consider what else is on your mind at the time, offer it to God, and then begin to listen again with open ears.

God offered Habakkuk guidance on hearing his voice:

What's God going to say to my questions? ...I'll climb to the lookout tower and scan the horizon. I'll wait to see what God says, how he'll answer my complaint. And then God answered: Write this. Write what you see. Write it out in big block letters, so that it can be read on the run.[222]

---

[221] I Sam. 3:9 [MSG].

According to this Scripture, Habakkuk followed these steps:

1. *He got alone with God.* Habakkuk retired to his watchtower to be alone. While at the watch-post, a watchman always needed to observe with an intent eye for everything in view. This represents the intensity in which we must focus on God. That will require a withdrawal from the things around us in order to focus on what is on God's mind. Even Jesus often went to solitary places when he needed to hear God's voice.[223]

2. *He waited.* Habakkuk not only prepared himself with an outward and inward silence, but he was willing to pause and wait for God to speak to him. Our present culture isn't comfortable with silence or waiting... and maybe we aren't either! "When we have prayed to God, we must observe what answers God gives by His Word, His Spirit, and His providences.[224]

3. *He wrote down what he had heard.* The Lord commanded Habakkuk to write down what he had heard which allowed it to be legible for anyone reading it. Journaling can be a helpful way to record what God is saying to you.

Proverbs offers advice about listening to God, "Listen for God's voice in everything you do, everywhere you go; he's the one who will keep you on track."[225]

---

[222] Hab. 2:1-3 [MSG].

[223] Matt. 14:23, Mark 1:35, Luke 4:42-44

[224] Jamieson, Robert, A.R. Fauset, and David Brown. (Oak Harbor, WA: Logos Research Systems, 1997).

[225] Prov. 3:6 [MSG].

Chapter 10

Journaling

Journaling can be one of the most powerful tools in our growth toward wholeness. Sometimes thoughts get locked inside of us and are difficult to sort out. Journaling is a helpful way to release them and examine them. In the process we gain insights that we would not have otherwise seen. "It also opens up new spaces within us of which we were not aware before we started to write."[226]

If in our writing we give descriptions and information about our daily life, we are creating a diary. Journaling can include descriptions, but it also contains reflections about what took place. It also expresses emotions and understanding about these happenings.

In addition, a spiritual journal is different from a regular journal. A spiritual journal is a written record of personal reactions to spiritual matters; and in the process of reflecting, the Holy Spirit can become our counselor.

Writing requires a great act of trust… (It is like) giving away the few loaves and fishes we have, trusting that they will multiply in the giving. Once we dare to 'give away' on paper the few thoughts that come to us, we start discovering how much is hidden underneath these thoughts and thus we gradually come in touch with our own riches and resources.[227]

---

[226] Henri Nouwen, *Spiritual Direction* (San Francisco: Harper Collins Publishers, 2006), 99.

[227] Ibid., 99.

"Spiritual writing has a very important place in spiritual formation... (it provides) a constant attempt to identify ways in which God is present among us."[228] As a formational tool, it can be used to record sermon notes, prayers, reflections, application of scripture, meaningful quotes from books or classics, ways God is present among us, and ways God is working in our lives. You can also use it in a practice called "Examen" in which you review the day, reflecting on where you have sensed God the most and where you have sensed him the least.

Journaling can be done by hand or by using a computer. However, typing on a keyboard tends to engage the mind; whereas, writing with the hand helps engage the heart. Since we write slower than we think, writing allows us to be more reflective. Also, writing with the hand tends to be a tactile experience with the words flowing from our mind, down our arm, into our hand and onto the page.

Helps on banishing your anxiety about journaling:

1. Write quickly and write everything you think, allowing the words to freely fall from your mind.
2. Avoid erasing any words. It takes time and distracts.
3. Do not worry about neatness or even grammar. Just get your thoughts and feelings on paper.
4. Try not to self-censor your writing; let go of 'shoulds' and just write what comes.
5. Accept whatever comes to mind and just write it.
6. Imagine Christ as your audience in this process!

"With any discipline...beginnings are awkward. Stay with it. Give it time and practice and the artificiality of the discipline will fade, giving way to familiarity and fluency."[229]

---

[228]Ibid., 98-99.

[229] Ibid., 105.

Chapter 11

Being Conformed to the Image of Christ

If we were honest, most of us would prefer to have our spiritual formation focused on those places in which we are more together. But being conformed to the image of Christ takes place in the areas where we are most unlike Christ, not yet conformed to his image. This is uncomfortable and becomes easy to avoid, especially when we feel incomplete and broken already.

However, through some means – Scripture, worship, prayer or another person – God will attempt to speak to us. As a disciple of Jesus, we will be asked to deny ourselves, take up our cross daily, follow him;[230] love Christ more than our dearest loved ones and even our own life;[231] obey what he commands;[232] love one another;[233] and bear much fruit.[234] Paul even tells us that we must be willing to be "crucified with Christ",[235] so that we no longer live but he lives in us.

What does it mean to be crucified with Christ? David Benner says that "what needs to be crucified are (our) ways of living apart from surrender to God's will."[236] Taking up our

---

[230] Matt. 16:24, Luke 9:23

[231] Luke 14:26

[232] Jn. 14:15, Jn. 8:31

[233] Jn. 13:34-35

[234] Jn. 15:8

[235] Gal. 2:20

[236] David G. Benner, *Sacred Companions: The Gift of Spiritual Friendship and Direction* (Downers Grove, IL: InterVarsity Press, 2002), 39.

cross has a similar meaning. It may seem like our cross is that difficult person or situation, but that is the wrong focus. Instead, "our cross is the point of our unlikeness to the image of Christ, where we must die to self in order to be raised by God into wholeness of life in the image of Christ *right there at that point*"[237] Once God brings to our attention a place in which we need to be more conformed to his image, our response needs to be yes to God.

However, God will never force this response on us; we must give him permission. Taking up our cross, then, becomes the response we make to God's challenge for us to become more like him. Once we have given God permission, there must be a consecration or surrender of ourselves to God at the point of our unlikeness to his image. God then can begin to work in us to help us grow into greater wholeness as we continue to practice the spiritual disciplines.

It is not thou that shapest God
it is God that shapest thee.
If thou art the work of God
await the hand of the artist
who does all things in due season.
Offer Him thy heart,
soft and tractable,
and keep the form
in which the artist has fashioned thee.
Let thy clay be moist,
lest thou grow hard
and lose the imprint of his fingers.
-St. Irenaeus

---

[237] Robert Mulholland, *Invitation to a Journey* (Downers Grove, IL: InterVarsity Press, 1993), 38.

GOING DEEPER ⇩

Reflection Questions *(for Individuals or a Group)*

CONNECTING WITH GOD
In silence, offer God anything that is on your mind that might
be a distraction to you. Then 'let it go' so you can concentrate
on God and what he wants to say to you right now. (Silently
pray a prayer of thanksgiving to God.)

THINKING OUTLOUD
Questions to Ponder or Discuss:
1. Begin the session by focusing on this object: Fill a jar with a
   little dirt and then water. Put on the lid and shake it up. Sit it
   nearby so you can observe it.
* Read Psalms 46:10 and reflect on this truth: "We have to be
  still long enough so the waters of our soul can become still
  and we are able to hear God."
* How long did it take for the water to become clear?

2. John Calvin said, "The Word of God is not received by faith if
   it flits about in the top of the brain, but when it takes root in
   the depth of the heart." Spirituality involves the head and the
   heart but it is easy to just settle for a relationship with God that
   involves our mind.
* Why is it easier to engage the mind as we read God's word
  rather than our heart?
* What are some ways we can involve both our head and heart
  in this process?
3. We would normally be concerned if someone we loved had no
   physical hungry. However, a lack of spiritual hunger should
   also be a concern.
   * What could be some reasons for a lack of appetite for
     spiritual nourishment?
   * What are some ways to increase our appetite?

75

4. Close your eyes and ponder these two situations: (a) You have just messed up big time. What does God's voice sound like to you right now? (b) You have just lost something very important to you. What are your feelings about God right now?
   - What does this say about your view of God?
   - What can you do to change your view of God?

5. Reflect on the triangle diagram (spirit, soul and body).
   - Discuss the reasons why (and the consequences of) the body or soul being in dominant position instead of spirit?
   - How can the spirit be maintained in the prominent position?

6. Reflect on the two categories of spiritual disciplines (abstinence or engagement). These can be compared to *breathing in and out* (both are obviously essential).
   - Which do you spend the most time doing? Least?
   - How can this affect your relationship with God?

7. Read the following thoughts about the discipline of Solitude:
   - "Without solitude we are dangerous in community." (Ruth Haley)
   - Solitude is the most radical of the disciplines for life in the spirit. Prison officials are aware of this and therefore use solitary confinement to break the strongest of wills. (Dallas Willard)
   - Solitude is difficult because it forces us to look at ourselves. So, we often choose to stay busy so that we don't have to face the many seductive visitors that pound on our door.
   - If we don't have a strong sense of who we are in Christ, we simply seem to lose our sense of self when there is no one to mirror back who we are. Without the oxygen of doing and the mirror of approval, our feelings of being real and important evaporate…These disconcerting feelings…reveal how much of our identity is embedded in a false sense of self. And they

show us how easy it is to avoid solitude because we dislike being unproductive and unapplauded. (Adele Calhoun)

- "When we are not finding ourselves loved by God in solitude, in the company of others we are always on the prowl for ways they can fill our emptiness. We enter life in community trying to grab and grasp from others what only God can give. (Ruth Haley)
  - Which thoughts troubled or challenged you the most from these quotes? Why?
  - Why do most people find it hard to spend time in solitude?
  - When do you struggle the most being alone?
  - Find five minutes each day this week to sit in solitude and silence. (If you get distracted, have some paper nearby to jot down things that come to your mind. Then return to your silence.) Try increasing your time in silence as the weeks go by. Reflect on your experience when you have done this for a week.

BEING FORMED BY THE WORD
Read Mark 1:35-38. *(Follow the instructions for "Spending time with Jesus" in Appendix B)*

- After doing the bible study, answer these questions: What did you discover about Jesus as you shared this experience with him?
- Why was solitude and silence a priority to Jesus?
- How would you respond if someone said to you, "Everyone is looking for you"? (Mark 1:37) Would you be tempted to give in to what they wanted you to do?

PRAYING FOR GOD'S HEART
Offer a prayer for what you are committed to doing this week.

TAKING TIME TO BE FORMED

First Day:

Make a timeline of your spiritual journey and reflect on it. What were your earliest spiritual stirrings? How has God tended to call you to growth over the course of your journey? Are you in a growing period right now?

Second Day:

1. Offer some time to God doing one of these practices. Then journal about your experience. (You may want to review some of the ideas in the section on journaling).

- *Silence*: Set a period of time in which you isolate yourself from other sounds (i.e. all media, TV, computer, phone, etc.). Avoid talking with your mouth or your mind and instead be attentive to the voice of Christ. What did you experience?

- *Solitude*: Spend fifteen to twenty minutes alone with God (with no other person present) with no agenda on your part. After the time is up, consider how it felt for you to be alone with God. Was it difficult or enjoyable? Did you sense him speaking to you in any way? Did you sense his presence or his love for you?

- *Simplicity*: Intentionally let go of something in your life. For example, clean out your garage, basement, a closet or the attic; give some of your things away; discontinue your cable TV; give up one of the activities you do; ride your bike or walk somewhere instead of driving your car. How did this activity make you aware of your own susceptible to the patterns of this culture?

- *Fasting*: Spend a week fasting in one of these ways: (2) Abstain from media [TV, radio, music, email, cell phones, computer games, etc.]; (3) Fast from sports, shopping, or reading; (4) Abstain from morning coffee, sodas or desserts. Offer some of the time you would have spent doing this activity to being with God. How has this experience of fasting been for you?

Third Day:

Draw a triangle on a piece of paper. Place the parts in the positions they are in your life right now (body, soul, and spirit). Which part is in the upward, authoritative position? What tips your triangle into another position? What needs to happen to allow your spirit to be placed in the position of priority?

Fourth Day:

Copy on some 3x5 cards words and scriptures about how God sees you (see the words in this section for help). Read these words every day for a month. Take turns meditating on different ones. Allow God to transform your "view of self" as you begin believing the truth about what he says about you!

Fifth Day:

Using the profile in Appendix A, compare your view of God as a child and your view of God now.
- Who were the most important influencers of your view of God during your childhood (parents, church/Sunday School teacher, peers, culture, media, etc.)?
- How does your view of God affect your relationship with God? Spend time looking up the scriptures about God's characteristics in Appendix A.

Bibliography

Barton, Ruth Haley. *Invitation to Solitude and Silence.* Downers Grove, IL: InterVarsity Press, 2004.

Benner, David. *Sacred Companions.* Downers Grove, IL: InterVarsity Press, 2002.

Bonhoeffer, Dietrich. *Life Together.* New York: Harper, 1954.

Bonhoeffer , Dietrich. *The Cost of Discipleship.* New York: Touchstone, 1995.

Calhoun, Adele Ahlberg. *Spiritual Disciples Handbook: Practices that Transform us.* Downers Grove, IL: InterVarsity Press, 2005.

Eldredge, John. *Waking the Dead.* Nashville: Thomas Nelson, 2003.

Foster, Richard. *Spiritual Formation: A Pastoral Letter.* Englewood, CO: Renovare, 2004.

Haley, Ruth. *Invitation to Solitude and Silence.* Downers Grove, IL: InterVarsity Press, 2004.

Jones, E. Stanley. *Conversion.* Nashville: Abingdon Press, 1959.

Jones, Tony. *The Sacred Way.* Grand Rapids, MI: Zondervan, 2004.

Mulholland, Robert. *Invitation to a Journey.* Downers Grove, IL: InterVarsity Press, 1993.

Nouwen, Henri. *The Way of the Heart.* New York: Ballantine Books, 1981.

Principe, Walter. *Exploring Christian Spirituality..* Edited by Kenneth J. Collins. Grand Rapids, MI: Baker Books, 2000.

Saunders, Stanley. "Learning Christ," *Interpretation* 56, no.2 (April 2002): 155-167.

Scazzero, Peter. *Emotionally Healthy Spirituality.* Nashville, TN: Thomas Nelson, 2006.

Underhill, Evelyn. *Concerning the InnerLife: Selected Writings of Evelyn Underhill.* Nashville: Upper Room Books, 1926.

Underhill, Evelyn. *The Soul's Delight: Selected Writings of Evelyn Underhill.* Nashville: Upper Room Books, 1926.

Vine, W.E. *Expository Dictionary of New Testament Words.* Grand Rapids, MI: Zondervan. 1982.

Additional Resources

Benner, David G. *Desiring God's Will: Aligning our Hearts with the Heart of God.* Downers Grove, IL: InterVarsity Press, 2005.

Blythe, Teresa. *50 Ways to Pray: Practices from Many Traditions and Times.* Nashville: Abingdon Press, 2006.

Creps, Earl and Dan Kimball. *Off-road Disciplines: Spiritual Adventures of Missional Leaders.* Hoboken, NJ: Jossey-Bass, 2006.

Curtis, Brent and John Eldredge. *The Sacred Romance: Drawing Closwer to the Heart of God.* Nashville: Thomas Nelson, 1997.

Demarest, Bruce. *Satisfy your Soul: Restoring the Heart of Christian Spirituality.* Colorado Springs: NavPress, 1999.

Foster, Richard. *Celebration of Discipline: The Path to Spiritual Growth.* NY: HarperOne, 1998.

Foster, Richard J. *Prayer: Finding the Heart's True Home.* San Francisco: HarperCollins Publishers, 1992.

Gemignani, Michael C. *Spiritual Formation for Pastors.* Elgin, IL, 2002.

Miller, Wendy. *Invitation to Presence: A Guide to Spiritual Disciplines.* Nashville: Upper Room Books, 2000.

Moore, Beth. *Praying God's Word: Breaking Free from Spiritual Strongholds.* Nashville: Broadman & Holman Publishers, 2000.

Shawchuck, Norman and Rueben P. Job. *A Guide to Prayer for All Who Seek God.* Nashville: Upper Room Books, 2003.

Tozer, A.W. *The Pursuit of God: The Human Thirst for the Divine.* Wheaton, IL: Tyndale House, 1982.

Whitney, Donald. *Spiritual Disciplines for the Christian Life.* Colorado Springs: NavPress, 1997.

Willard, Dallas. *Renovation of the Heart: Putting on the Character of Christ.* Colorado Springs: NavPress, 2002.

Wright, H. Norman. *Simplify your Life and Get More Out of It!* Wheaton, IL: Tyndale House Publishers, 1998.

Part III

HOLY AND WHOLE in Body

Don't you realize that your body is the temple of the Holy Spirit, who lives in you and was given to you by God? You do not belong to yourself, for God bought you with a high price. So you must honor God with your body.
-I Corinthians 6:18-20 [NLT]

Our bodies have now become the Bethlehem of Jesus.
Jesus lives in us and takes up residence within.
-Oswald Chambers

Could it be that our bodies reflect more accurately what we believe than our actual words? Oswald maintains that "we are a walking theological statement before we open our mouths. But most of us don't take our bodies very seriously."[238]

St. Augustine said "Men go abroad to admire the heights of mountains, the mighty billows of the sea, the broad tides of rivers, the compass of the ocean and the circuits of the stars. Yet they ignore the wonder found in themselves."[239]

Let's stop now and take time to wonder! How does that wonder prompt us in caring for ourselves physically?

---

[238] Roy Oswald, *Clergy Self-Care* (Herndon, VA: Alban Institute, 1991), 16.

[239] St. Augustine, *Confessions of St. Augustine*: The Modern English Version (Grand Rapids, MI: Revell, 2008), 165.

Chapter 12

Differing Opinions about the Body

The body is generally seen as an object with physical properties, such as skin, weight, solidness, and substance; but the word "physical" has also acquired social, spiritual, and metaphysical meanings.[240]

Throughout the ages, there have been differing opinions about the body. Ancient Greek philosophers saw the body as carnal and weak, but saw the mind and spirit as highly exalted. They also saw the body as something to be contended with, like leprosy. In comparison, for the early Hebrews the body was not something to be used and disposed of, but something that remained immortal.

There are a number of places in the Old Testament where God allows us to see his perception of us. After God created man, he utters the words "it was very good".[241] The Psalmist also speaks of the goodness of what God has created, saying "You knit me together in my mother's womb. I praise you because I am fearfully and wonderfully made; your works are wonderful."[242] This goodness includes our physical bodies, created with precision and amazing complexities.

In the New Testament the Greek word *sarx* is closely parallel to the Old Testament word for flesh, *basar*. Sarx is sometimes used in the New Testament to indicate our sinful flesh or sinful nature.[243] It is referred to by Jesus as weak

---

[240] S.V. McCasland, *The Interpreter's Dictionary of the Bible* (Nashville: Abingdon Press, 1962).

[241] Gen. 1:27-31

[242] Ps. 139:13-14

[243] Gal. 5:13, 16; 6:8

87

when he says, "The spirit is willing but the flesh *(sarx)* is weak."[244]

In the gospels, another Greek word for body is *soma* and usually refers to the external man. Paul told Timothy that "bodily *(somatike)* exercise profits a little, but godliness is profitable for all things, having promise of the life that now is and of that which is to come."[245] In this passage the body seems to be subordinated beneath, or lesser than, the spiritual virtue of godliness.

Paul uses the imagery of an athlete to compare with the challenge of living for Christ and speaks of the body in this way, "I beat my body and make it my slave so that after I have preached to others, I myself will not be disqualified for the prize."[246]

Paul grieves over the reality that "as long as we are at home in the body we are away from the Lord."[247] He regrets that life in this body here on earth prevented him from being fully present with the Lord. Nevertheless, he says, "to live is Christ, and to die is gain."[248] In other words, bodily existence is important, but only if we use it to glorify God and not ourselves.

Metaphorically, Paul refers to the Church as the "body of Christ" of which Christ is the head[249] He compares the unity and diversity of the physical body with the unity God desires in the body of Christ, his church. Using bodily terms, the foot, the hand, the ear, the eye, and the head, he demonstrates the

---

[244] Matt. 26:41, Mark 14:38

[245] I Tim. 4:8 [NKJ].

[246] I Cor. 9:27

[247] II Cor. 5:6

[248] Phil. 1:21

[249] Romans 12:4-5, I Cor. 12:12-27

need to respect every part of the body as important.[250] This must certainly be true for both the body of Christ, as well as our physical bodies, which he made with purpose and design!

The greatest value that Paul assigns to our bodies is as a residence or dwelling place for God's temple.[251] His penetrating words challenge our view of our bodies, "Do you not know that your body is a temple of the Holy Spirit, who is in you whom you have received from God?[252] In other words, our bodies are the garage for our souls, a temporary parking place while here on earth.[253]

Even though some of the saints throughout the years practiced mortification of their bodies (lengthy fasting, sleep deprivation, poverty, and going without eating to the detriment of their own physical health), Julian of Norwich, one such saint, challenges us with these words, "One should not despise one's bodily life. Rather one is obliged to regard one's body as good and to hold it in honor, since God has created it and will raise it up on the last day."[254]

Our bodies are an amazing creation of God. The function of every cell and every system in our body follows an intricate DNA blueprint. Simmons, a physician who has studied the body for 40 years, says the "interior of the human body is a "much busier place than New York City, London, Mexico

---

[250] I Cor. 12:15-22

[251] I Cor. 3:16

[252] I Cor. 6:19

[253] Deborah Newman, *Comfortable in your own Skin: Making Peace with your Body Image* (Carol Stream, IL: Tyndale House Publishers, 2007).

[254] Quoted in *Earth Prayers*, ed. Elizabeth Roberts and Elias Amidon (San Francisco: Harpers, 1991), 251, originally from *Meditation with Meister Eckhart* by Matthew Fox (Santa Fe, M: Bear & Company, 1983).

City, Tokyo, and Bombay combined."[255] In his book, *What Darwin Didn't Know,* he summarizes the amazing body that God has created with these words,

> Ten to seventy-five trillion cells participate in more than a quadrillion purposeful chemical interactions each day that help us walk, breathe, think, sleep, procreate, see, hear, smell, feel, digest food, eliminate waste, write, read, talk, make red cells, remove dead cells, fight infections, behave, misbehave, absorb nutrients, transport oxygen, eliminate carbon dioxide, maintain balance, carry on dialogue, understand instructions, argue, and make complex decisions, just to name a few common activities.[256]

Is there any doubt that God deeply cares about our physical bodies since he made them with such intricate design? He also wants us to care about them too, expressing it in the way that we "care for" them.

---

[255] Geoffrey Simmons, *What Darwin Didn't Know* (Eugene, OR: Harvest House Publishers, 2004).

[256] Ibid., 16.

Chapter 13

Body Check-Up

Take some time to evaluate your commitment to physical wholeness. Answer yes or no to the following questions:

1. Do you avoid regular exercise or struggle in making it a regular routine in your life?
2. Are you more than ten pounds overweight?
3. Do you drink less than 6-8 glasses of water a day?
4. Does your diet regularly include some of these: sugar, salt, white flour, saturated fats or artificial sweeteners?
5. Do you consume soft drinks on a regular basis?
6. Do you eat fast food, packaged meals, or processed foods on a regular basis?
7. Has it been more than two years since you've had a physical checkup?
8. Do you take over-the-counter remedies more than once a month? (i.e. aspirin, Tylenol, antacids, bowel softeners, products for diarrhea, sleeping aids, etc.)
9. Do you often feel exhausted before noon?
10. Do you sleep less than 7-8 hours a night?
11. Do you get sick frequently?
12. Do you have trouble saying no?
13. Do you tend to do too much, or work long hours?
14. Do you take work or worry home with you?
15. Do you rarely take a Sabbath day of rest and relaxation?

Take an additional look at any question you have answered with a "Yes" for it may indicate an issue in the area of your physical wholeness.

During my childhood the church I attended, in direct and indirect ways, taught me that the only thing that mattered was the spiritual dimension. I observed numerous ways in which the physical body was neglected and disregarded as unimportant (food offered at church socials; constant intake of substances, such as caffeine, sugar and salt; lack of information or modeling of the importance of exercise; and the obvious number of overweight members). I even had a pastor's wife who boasted about getting only 4-5 hours of sleep a night, who unfortunately died at an early age.

I now realize that during my 20s, 30s, and 40s I violated a number of the principles in the "Body Check-Up". I did not exercise on a regular basis and I failed to drink enough water. I was a workaholic and busy all the time. I had poor boundaries and often had a difficult time saying no. At some point, I began experiencing physical problems such as allergies, indigestion, constipation, candida, and back and neck problems. I tried to fix these issues through reading self-help books and healthy living books, practicing natural health, embracing alternative methods of healing, taking vitamins, and crazily controlling the things that went into my mouth. At one time, I had over one hundred books on health.

Eventually, I came to a crisis that caused me to have to address some of the emotional and spiritual issues of my life. As I addressed these issues, I noticed my physical health improving as well. God began to change me in ways I could never have changed on my own. I became peaceful and balanced, and people told me that they noticed the difference. And all of this made amazing changes in my physical body as well!

The fact that there is a correlation between a person's physical health and their sense of mental and emotional well-being has been well-documented. Disease occurs when we do not take care of ourselves, when we fail to realize the inter-relationships of the emotional, physical, mental, and spiritual parts of ourselves. Accepting this principle will mean that we will act in a way that demonstrates care for our entire being, including our physical bodies.

Chapter 14

Stewardship of the Body

What does the care of our physical bodies entail? It usually involves attention to such things as proper diet and nutrition, drinking plenty of water, exercise, proper breathing, and Sabbath rest, as well as enough sleep each night.

We are told that Americans are doing poorly in most of these areas, compared to other countries in the world. We are bombarded by fast food restaurants on every corner, as well as constant ads for junk food from every possible media. "It's easier to find a Snickers bar, a Big Mac or a Coke than it is to find an apple"[257] on the streets of our cities. Even magazines thought of as wholesome reading, such as *Family Doctor* and *National Geographic Kids*, are filled with pages of ads for heavily sugared cereals, snacks, soda, and fast foods. Scientists and food activists at Yale University call this a "toxic food environment".[258]

In addition, studies show that even Christian leaders pay little attention to these areas of physical wholeness. In 1987 a study on clergy, ages thirty-five to fifty, revealed that 94% had no defined fitness program, 78% were overweight by sixteen pounds or more and 89% admitted to having poor eating habits.[259]

Another study that took place over the past 30 years revealed that the health of clergy in the United Methodist denomination was greatly deteriorating. It found that the

---

[257] T. Colin Campbell and Thomas Campbell, *The China Study* (Dallas, TX: BenBella Books, 2006), xvii.

[258] Ibid, xvii.

[259] Roy Oswald, *Clergy Self-Care* (Herndon, VA: Alban Institute, 1991).

majority of United Methodist clergy worked 60-70 hours a week, were 15-20 pounds overweight, exercised less than 30 minutes each week, reported gastro-intestinal discomfort on a regular basis, took one or more prescription medications on an ongoing basis, were in the "high-risk" category for heart-related problems, and reported low morale and/or exhaustion.[260] What must this lack of physical self-care be communicating to others in their sphere of influence?

Unfortunately, too many Christians see physical self-care as optional, as if it were irrelevant to their relationship with God and their influence on others. Oswald offers a different viewpoint when he states, "I take care of myself, not only for my sake, or in gratitude for the life given me by God, but also for the sake of others."[261]

When stated that way, the issue of physical health and self-care becomes a matter of biblical stewardship. Unfortunately, the culture is often more interested than Christians themselves in promoting good health. A case in point is the United States Army. They believe that the qualities that make a good chaplain in the army are self-discipline, initiative, confidence, intelligence, *physical fitness*, the ability to perform under pressure, leadership, the ability to make decisions quickly, and respect for subordinates. Note that physical fitness is listed as a key quality, along with self-discipline.[262] Why should we, as Christians, not learn from the priorities that are essential for Army Chaplains? The battle we wage is even more challenging than the one the military fights. Should we not be prepared to give it our best?

---

[260] The United Methodist Church, "Interpreter Online," http://www.interpretermagazine.org [accessed July 8, 2008].

[261] Roy Oswald, *Clergy Self-Care* (Herndon, VA: Alban Institute, 1991), 6.

[262] National Guard. Career and Job Skills. http:www.nationalguard.com [accessed June 24, 2011].

It will not be easy to practice principles of good health. As Christians we have allowed ourselves to be influenced by advertisers and the practices of our culture. Most of us live at a fast pace and "eat on the run", tending to eat for our own pleasure and comfort more often than we realize.

Pleasing others, looking good, guilt or fear, and feeling good about ourselves will never be enough motivation for a lasting change for our physical health. Even diets, self-will, determination, and accountability will not bring about the change we hope for in this area. The only real motivation that will help us change the habits of our physical body (regular exercise, proper diet, losing weight, and getting enough rest) is a love for God and desire to honor and please him.

In order to change, we must begin by personally answering the following questions. Does physical self-care really matter to God? Is our Christian influence compromised by how we care for our physical bodies? Do we live as if our bodies really belong to us instead of God?

Proper Diet

The statistics indicate a weight problem for both adults and children in this country. Two out of three adults are overweight and one-third of the adult population is obese. In addition about 15% of youth (six to nineteen) are overweight and one third are either overweight or at risk of becoming overweight.[263] The Get America Fit Foundation reports that being overweight greatly increases the risks of many health issues: breast cancer, heart disease, Type II diabetes, sleep apnea, gallbladder disease, osteoarthritis, colon cancer, hypertension, and strokes.

In his documentary, "Super-Size Me", Morgan Spurlock took on the challenge of eating McDonald's food every meal for one month to see what would happen. He ate everything on

---

[263] Ibid.

McDonald's menu at least once and would supersize his meals if asked. What was the outcome? Well, it took only three days for him to start to feel the effects of a total McDonald's diet. Before long, he had gained over 25 pounds and by the third week of his month-long experiment, his doctors were urging him to quit as his health had become so poor that he was liable to suffer long-term damage.[264]

This documentary also included an experiment Spurlock did where he placed McDonald's French fries in a jar on a countertop. In a month's time the fries had no mold on them (mold will occur on food that is living and nutritious) and had not broken down in any way. How could the fries break down in your own body and pass on nutritional value to you if they could not break down in a month without refrigeration? Spurlock learned that you can lighten your load by steering clear of fast food and by opting instead for lots of fresh fruit and vegetables and Whole grain foods.

Does the Bible guide us in what to eat? In Genesis, God offers these foods to Adam and Eve for their daily sustenance, "I have given you every herb bearing seed, which is upon the face of all the earth, and every tree, in which is the fruit of a tree yielding seed; to you it shall be for meat."[265] This indicates that their meals consisted of fruits and vegetables, herbs and seed bearing plants (nuts, beans, legumes, grains). In other words, their protein was plant based. However, after they sinned, God offered the first animal sacrifice and soon we began seeing references to animals for sacrifice and for food.[266]

Later in the Old Testament, we find Daniel and his three friends (Shadrach, Meshach, and Abednego) with a resolve

---

[264] Mark McLeod, "2004 Super Size Me," UGO Entertainment, http://www.celebritywonder.com/movie/2004_Super_Size_Me.html [accessed on July 8, 2008].

[265] Gen. 1:29 [KJV].

[266] Gen.4:4, 9:3-4

96

not to defile themselves with the food and wine of the Babylonians. What was the food they refused? In the first chapter of Daniel it is referred to as the king's meat,[267] the royal food,[268] or rich and dainty food.[269] Daniel asks the official to test him and his three friends for ten days while eating only vegetables and water, and then to compare their appearance with that of the young men who ate the royal food.[270] The results were surprising to the official, "At the end of the ten days they looked healthier and better nourished than any of the young men who ate the royal food."[271] One thing we do know is that their vegetable-based diet was better than the rich foods of the king (possibly foods such as: rich desserts, cheeses, fat-laden foods, and the unclean meats that God had forbidden.[272]

Some of the latest research indicates that "a good diet is the most powerful weapon we have against disease and sickness".[273] Campbell[274] sums up the latest findings of the most reputable scientific journals:

- Dietary change can enable diabetic patients to go off their medication.
- Heart disease can be reversed with diet alone.

---

[267] Dan. 1:13 [KJV].

[268] Dan. 1:8, 13 [NIV].

[269] Dan. 1:8, 13 [AMP].

[270] Dan. 1:12-13

[271] Dan. 1:15

[272] Lev. 11:1-20

[273] Colin Campbell and Thomas Campbell, *The China Study* (Dallas, TX: BenBella Books, 2006), 3.

[274] Ibid.

- Breast cancer is related to levels of female hormones in the blood, which are determined by the food we eat.
- Consuming dairy foods can increase the risk of prostate cancer.
- Antioxidants, found in fruits and vegetables, are linked to better mental performance in old age.
- Kidney stones can be prevented by a healthy diet.
- Type I diabetes, one of the most devastating diseases that can befall a child, is convincingly linked to infant feeding practices.

Colin Campbell is an advocate of a plant-based diet and in his book *The China Study*[275] he makes a strong case for the relationship between diet and disease. His conclusions are startling and his suggested plant-based diet would seem to be comparable to the food that God offered Adam and Eve in the garden.[276]

Since food is such an important factor to our physical health, it would be fitting to us all to begin to pay attention to what we eat. Statistics tell us that America's health is failing even though we spend more, per capita, on health care than any other country in the world ($2.3 trillion annually). Currently, "75 percent of healthcare costs are accounted for by chronic diseases, such as heart disease, diabetes, prostate cancer, breast cancer, and obesity."[277] Approximately two thirds of us are overweight, more of us are getting diabetes than ever before, and the War on Cancer has been a miserable failure.[278]

---

[275] Ibid.

[276] Gen. 1:29

[277] S. Keehan, *"Health Spending Projections through 2017"* (Health Affairs Web Exclusive W146, February 2008).

[278] Ibid.

Did you know that you are what you eat? "Your body craves natural food. Food that is processed, packaged or filled with additives, preservatives and sugar cannot be used by your body, thereby causing harm".[279]

Essentially, we are what we ingest, and the sugary colas, coffee drinks, and artificial "juices" are just as bad as the newest, fatty burger creation from the fast food joint down the street. Dousing your organs and cells with these beverages is not allowing them to properly function and attain optimal operations. If a fish cannot survive in a bowl filled with those types of beverages, what makes you think your cells can?[280]

But as Christians we have been taught by our culture that convenience and speed are important and essential to our lifestyle. But, in the long run, they offer only a substitute for what is real and truly healthy. We are being deceived because God never intended for our bodies to subsist on processed and chemical enriched foods even if they are most convenient to obtain.

Due to the fast-paced world we live in, most consumers believe it is easier to visit their local McDonalds or Burger King to partake in a greasy helping of chemicals and preservatives. Our bodies were not created to run off of French fries and Krispy Kreme donuts, and this new

---

[279] This information came from a handout from Maximized Living.

[280] Maximized Living, "*Health Essential #3: Maximum Quality Nutrition,*" http://www.maximizedliving.com/NutritionDetox/ MaximizedQualityNutrition.aspx [accessed August 1, 2011].

99

diet of convenience is posing a serious threat to healthy cell life![281]

According to Juice Plus, the latest research indicates that people can "improve their chances of living longer, healthier lives by eating more fruits and vegetables."[282] Fruits and vegetables offer your body a host of benefits - vitamins, minerals, anti-oxidants, fiber, and a better chance at avoiding cancer. According to the American Institute for Cancer research, diets that contain substantial and varied amounts of fruits and vegetables may potentially prevent 20 percent or more of the cases of cancer each year.

In addition to eating more fruits and vegetables, we need to stay away from refined and processed foods (i.e. white bread, white rice, white pasta, chips, etc.). These types of foods lack fiber, are full of empty calories, and will add pounds to a person's body.

Food supplies us with both nutrients and calories (energy).

The key to permanent weight loss (and proper functioning of the immune system) is to eat predominantly those foods that have a high proportion of nutrients (noncaloric food factors) to calories (carbohydrates, fats, and proteins)...Eating large quantities of high-nutrient foods is the secret to optimal health and permanent weight control.[283]

In other words, nutrient-dense foods are those foods that provide substantial amounts of vitamins and minerals and

---

[281] Ibid.

[282] Juice Plus+, www.juiceplus.com [accessed August 2, 2011].

[283] Joel Fuhrman, *Eat to Love* (Boston: Little Brown and Company, 2003), 7.

relatively few calories. Fruits, vegetables, and legumes are the most "nutrient-dense" foods available. Meat, dairy, refined grains, refined oils and refined sweets are the least "nutrient-dense". Fuhrman believes 90% of our daily diet should be comprised of nutrient-dense foods[284].

What foods rank the highest and the lowest in nutrient-density (ANDI Scores)? Some of the highest are: kale and collards (1000), other vegetables (between 160-820), fruits (between 60-212), and nuts (between 34-48). Some of the lowest are: cola (1), French fries (7), vanilla ice cream (9), cheddar cheese and potato chips (11), white bread and pasta (18), and beef and milk (20).

Sugary foods are not only low in nutrients, but also one of the leading contributors to disease in our culture today. The average American consumes 170 pounds of sugar each year, compared to 10 pounds two hundred years ago. Unfortunately, sugar contributes to a multitude of health problems. Begin reading labels as you shop so that you are aware of all the hidden sugar that is contained in products that you buy at the grocery store every week.

This quiz found in a book by Maximized Living[285] can help you find out where you stand in regard to healthy eating habits.

1. Do you eat out more than three times per week?
2. Do you eat boxed food more than twice a week?
3. Do you drink any type of soft drinks?
4. Do you eat less than five servings of vegetables per day?
5. Do you drink less than four glasses of water per day?
6. Do you feel "addicted" to certain foods?
7. Do you typically opt for lower-fat and lower calorie foods when given the choice?

---

[284] Dr. Fuhrman, *"For Superior Health and your Ideal Weight,"* http://www.drfuhrman.com [accessed August 2, 2011].

[285] B.J. Hardick, Kimberly Roberto, and Ben Lerner, *MaximizedLiving Nutrition Plans* (Celebration, FL: Maximized Living, 2009), 26-27.

8. Do you eat white flour, white rice, or white bread?
9. Do you use artificial sweeteners or consume foods that contain them?
10. Do you eat fried foods more than once a week?
11. Do you eat processed "deli" meat, bacon, sausage, or hot dogs?
12. Do you think that you get all your needed nutrients from food and therefore pass on any type of supplement?
13. Do you use vegetable oils in cooking or in salad dressings?
14. Do you use margarine?
15. Are most of the fruits and vegetables you eat conventionally grown (non-organic)?
16. Do you consume milk or dairy products?
17. Do you eat animal products more than twice a week?
18. Do you consider price and convenience of food to be more important than nutritional quality?
19. Do you eat sweets or candy more than once per week?
20. Do you consume alcoholic beverages more than 2-3 times a week?
21. Do you eat while rushed or under stress?
22. Do you, your doctor, or family think that you need to lose some body fat (weight)?
23. Do you have irregular blood sugar, diabetes, or pre-diabetes?
24. Do you have blood pressure over 120/80?
25. Do you suffer from sinus conditions, asthma, or allergies?
26. Do you have gastrointestinal concerns?
27. Do you frequently experience fatigue or insomnia?
28. Do you have emotional/mental challenges or trouble concentrating?
29. Do you suffer from joint pain or muscle aches?
30. Do you have hormonal imbalances?

Total up the number of items you said "Yes" to: _____

As you may have guessed, Maximized Living considers ALL of the items on this list as problematic when it comes to being healthy.[286] They prefer that you avoid answering yes to most of the questions. However, they offer the following score results:

0-5 GREAT
6-10 GOOD (but not the best)
11-15 NEEDS IMPROVEMENT
16-20 PRE-DISEASE
21+ CRISIS

Dr. Katie Benson[287], the author's personal chiropractic doctor, names these as the five most toxic foods: (1) processed meats (nitrates), (2) almost all fast foods, (3) soft drinks/diet pop, (4) packaged foods, (5) doughnuts, cookies, and white bread.

Whole grains offer better nutritional value than grains stripped of their nutritional contents (bran and germ). There are quite a variety of grains and flours available in their whole grain form: oat, barley, wheat, brown rice, rye, spelt, millet, quinoa, amaranth, triticale, teff, sorghum, garbanzo, hemp, and flours made from almonds and flax seed. Why not enjoy the variety of tastes from all these wonderful whole grains and flours, instead of grains stripped of their nutritional value!

Animal protein and dairy products increase the acid load in the body. The body then uses calcium in order to neutralize the acid. This calcium "ends up being pulled from the bones, and the calcium loss weakens them, putting them at greater risk for fracture."[288] Try substituting milk with options such as unsweetened almond milk, rice milk, or coconut milk.

---

[286] Ibid.

[287] Dr. Katie Benson practices holistic health principles in her Maximized Living practice in Marysville, OH. This information was gleamed from a workshop Dr. Benson led in June 2010.

[288] Campbell and Campbell, 205.

Use products such as almond butter or Earth Balance natural buttery spread in place of margarine. If you choose to use butter, buy organic butter instead of margarine.

Disease thrives in an acidic environment. The internal environment of our bodies is best maintained at a pH just above 7.0 which is considered alkaline and will be one of our best defenses against disease.[289] Some of the causes of an acidic environment within our bodies are stress, inflammation, high fat and protein foods, empty caloric foods (i.e. processed foods, sugar, artificial sweeteners, salt and fried foods). To find out the overall pH balance (or imbalance) of your body, test your saliva or urine with pH diagnostic test strips.[290] Charts that indicate foods that are acidic or alkaline can be helpful in making healthy food choices.[291]

Alkaline-type foods	Acidic-type foods
Most fruits (tomatoes and citrus fruits have an acid flavor but form alkaline residues)	Fruits that are acidic: dry fruit, cranberry, coconut, plum, pomegranate
Most vegetables, including root vegetables (potato, sweet potato, beets, parsnip, turnip), all types of squash	Vegetables that are acidic: green pea, snow pea, and most legumes (pinto, navy, lima, chickpea, kidney, soybean), commercial corn

[289] Russell Jaffe, *Food & Chemical Effects on Acid / Alkaline Body Chemical Balance,*" http://www.perque.com/HSC_AcidAlkChart_7-07FINAL.pdf [accessed August 1, 2011].

[290] pHion Balance, *"pHion Diagnostic pH Test Strips,"* http://www.phionbalance.com/ph-balancing-products/ph+test [accessed August 1, 2011]. This is a good online store in which to purchase pH test strips.

[291] Here is an online chart that I have found helpful: http://www.perque.com/HSC_AcidAlkChart_7-07FINAL.pdf [accessed August 1, 2011]. The acid/alkaline foods listed above come from this chart.

Nuts (cashew, almond) and most seeds	Pecan, brazil nut, pistachio, walnut and peanut (a legume)
Duck eggs, human milk	All meat, dairy, cheese and eggs
Water, herb tea, green tea, apple cider vinegar, sea salt, herbs and most spices	Sugar, artificial sugar, coffee, black tea, salt

We will all eat some acidic-type foods at times. Nevertheless, if you make alkaline-type foods your main emphasis and balance the acidic-type foods you eat with plenty of alkaline-type choices, you will have a predominately alkaline diet which is essential to a healthy body.

Eating less food also has health benefits. This can be challenging because today's trend is for restaurants to offer larger portions of food. If you have a tendency to eat everything on your plate, you may want to try ordering the smaller portion offered at many restaurants or take some home for later. It is best to avoid smorgasbords and family style meals. When eating at home, make it a practice to fill your plate only once.

Michael Pollan has written a small book entitled, *Food Rules*.[292] He gives a number of rules that can be guidelines for healthy eating.

- Avoid food products that contain high-fructose corn syrup.
- Avoid foods that have some form of sugar listed among the top three ingredients.
- Avoid food products containing ingredients that a third-grader cannot pronounce.
- Avoid foods with the word "lite", "low-fat" or "nonfat" in their names.

---

[292] Michael Pollan, *Food Rules: An Eater's Manual* (New York:Penguin Group, 2009).

- Avoid foods you see advertised on television (with a few exceptions). Only the biggest food manufacturers can afford to advertise their products on television.
- Shop the peripheries of the supermarket and stay out of the middle.
- Eat only foods that will eventually rot.
- It's not food if it's called by the same name in every language (i.e. Big Mac, Cheetos, or Pringles, etc.)
- Treat meat as a flavoring or special occasion food (instead of your main course).
- Eat sweet foods as you find them in nature.
- Don't eat breakfast cereals that change the color of the milk.
- The whiter the bread the worse it is for your health. Eat whole grains instead.
- Eat less. Scientific evidence indicates that eating less leads to better health and longer life.

Calorie restriction has repeatedly been shown to slow aging in animals, and many researchers believe it offers the single strongest link between diet and cancer prevention. We eat much more than our bodies need to be healthy, and the excess wreaks havoc…We are the first people in history to grapple with the special challenges posed by food abundance.[293]

So, how can you know when to stop eating? The Japanese say to stop when you are 80 percent full; people in India advise eating until you are 75 percent full; the Chinese specify 70 percent; and the French suggest not asking yourself 'Am I full', but 'Is my hunger gone'.[294] Another suggestion is to wait 15-20 minutes before you take in additional food. By then you

---

[293] Ibid., 101.

[294] Ibid.

will know if you are still hungry since your food has had time to properly inform your stomach! My mother suggests that you ask yourself, "Am I hungry enough to eat something healthy"? If not, you are eating for some other reason than hunger – entertainment, comfort, a reward, boredom or an addiction to a substance (sugar, caffeine, salt, fats, natural and artificial flavors, etc.).[295]

It might seem impossible in this culture to eat healthy, especially at public gatherings, church potlucks, and family events. However, it is a matter of balance, not perfection. Try keeping junk foods out of your diets at home and use good common sense when you are eating out in public. Try concentrating on foods in their natural form, as God made them, as often as possible. When you cut out refined sugar and empty carbohydrates from your diet, your body will more easily tell you what is not good for you. Once out of your system, these foods will seem too sweet or make you feel sick because your body is not used to them. After awhile you will no longer desire them.

The Value of Drinking Water

Plenty of clean fresh water is essential for life. "It is a powerful and critical resource that our cells need in order to survive".[296] It is second only to oxygen in importance to the body's functioning. You can live for several months without food, but you can only live for a little over a week without water for your body is composed of approximately 70 percent

---

[295] In order to understand food addiction, try putting the words "Why McDonald's Fries Taste so Good" in your search engine or try reading Eric Schlosser's book, *Fast Food Nation.*

[296] Maximized Living, *"Power Episode #38: One of the Most Critical Resources for our Bodies,"* http://www.maximizedliving.com/ Home/MaximizedLivingBlog/tabid/772/Article/311/Default.aspx [accessed August 3, 2011].

water.[297] "Every system in your body depends on water. Water flushes toxins out of vital organs, carries nutrients to your cells and provides a moist environment for ear, nose and throat tissues. Every day you lose water through your breath, perspiration, urine and bowel movements".[298] That's why water should be your primary beverage throughout every day. Cola, coffee, teas, and processed fruit juice are not satisfactory substitutes for water.

Consider this information about "Water Facts"[299]:

- Lack of water is the number one trigger of daytime fatigue.
- Your body loses as much water when you are asleep as when you are awake.
- Your body needs as much water in cold weather as it does in warm weather.
- A mere 2 percent drop in body water can trigger brain fog and short-term memory impedance.
- Drinking five glasses of water daily decreases the risk of colon cancer by 45 percent, breast cancer by 79 percent, and bladder cancer by 50 percent.

Water is involved in nearly every body process – digestion, absorption, circulation, and elimination and an insufficient amount can be related to a number of ailments including chronic constipation, hemorrhoids, varicose veins, urinary

---

[297] Stormie Omartian, *Greater Health God's Way* (Eugene, OR: Harvest House Publishers, 1996).

[298] Dr. Katie Benson, *"Have you had your Fill?* Handout received from Maximized Living, Marysville, OH on March 7, 2011.

[299] B.J. Hardick, Kimberly Roberto, and Ben Lerner, *MaximizedLiving Nutrition Plans* (Celebration, FL: Maximized Living, 2009), 66.

tract infections, and kidney stones."[300] Lack of water can also contribute to excess body fat, poor muscle tone, digestive problems, poor brain functioning, as well as many others conditions. [301] Unfortunately, as we age our sense of thirst becomes dulled. That's why it's important to drink water even when you do not feel thirsty.

So how much water should we drink each day? One suggestion is the 8 by 8 rule (drink eight 8-ounce glasses of water). Another rule of thumb says to divide your weight (in pounds) by two. The resulting number is the number of ounces of water you need each day. For example, if you weigh 150 pounds, you should drink 75 ounces of water a day.[302]

The best source for water comes from mineral, filtered, distilled, sparkling, and artesian well water. Drinking   from safe containers is also important. Plastic bottles require petroleum and other chemicals for creation and toxins can leach into the water from the plastic bottle[303], especially if you freeze the bottled water, it sits in a hot car, or the bottle is reused. Instead, try refillable stainless-steel bottles or glass.

---

[300] Linda Rector Page, *Healthy Healing,* 10th Ed. (Healthy Healing Pub. www.healthyhealing.com. 1997), 186.

[301] Phyllis Balch, *Prescription for Nutritional Healing,* 3rd Ed. (N. Bergen, NJ: The Vitamin Shoppe, 2000).

[302] WikiHow, *How to Drink More Water Every Day,"* http://www.wikihow.com/Drink-More-Water-Every-Day [accessed August 1, 2011].

[303] Maximized Living, *"Power Episode #38: One of the Most Critical Resources for our Bodies,"* http://www.maximizedliving.com/ Home/MaximizedLivingBlog/tabid/772/Article/311/Default.aspx [accessed August 3, 2011].

Exercise

Think about this: The longest lived peoples in human history usually walked everywhere they went. Years ago, exercise was just a part of a person's daily routine and not a separate activity. As they worked the land or walked wherever they went, they were getting plenty of exercise. However, we live a more sedentary life and the jobs and tasks we do generally do not involve physical exercise. That creates a lifestyle in which exercise must become a separate activity or it does not happen.

The lack of physical exercise is considered by doctors in the United States to be the most serious health hazard we face. It is said that a person needs at least twenty minutes of exercise three times a week to keep their cardiovascular systems healthy.

Moderate exercise can help lower blood pressure, can lower one's chance for certain cancers, can counter the effects of aging, stimulates bone and muscle tissue, gives you energy, and can help with weight control. Exercise can also elevate your mood, giving you the positive effects of increased endorphins. It makes your heart stronger by pumping more blood with less effort, lowers cholesterol and blood pressure, prevents and controls diabetes, strengthens bones and muscles, and controls weight. A study published in the Archives of Internal Medicine showed that participants who had moderate to high exercise routines lived 1.3 to 3.7 years longer than those who seldom exercised.

Even though we know it is good for us, most of us find it hard to incorporate exercise into our daily lives as a habit. When the merits of exercise are expounded, I can hear you say, "But I hate exercise" or "I just cannot find the time to exercise" or "I cannot keep up the habit of exercising." For years, I too found it challenging to be consistent with exercise. When people talked about the need to do it, I felt guilty and wanted to ignore what they said. It took a personal crisis, along with a physical health crisis, to motivate me to begin changing in this aspect of my life.

You might try combining a physical exercise with a spiritual discipline. For instance, walking and meditating (or praying). There is also great benefit from an exercise called the "Surge". Surge Training[304] is a great way to achieve maximum benefit within minimal time, pushing your body to its maximum potential.

This is what you do as you Surge. Start with a few gentle stretches. Then do six exercises (one after the other) for one minute a piece (total of six minutes). Some ideas for exercises is running in place, running on a treadmill, stationary bike, jumping rope, arm circles, mini-trampoline, jumping jacks, leg lifts, pushups, etc. You should use maximum effort for every second of the surge. After six exercises, rest for one minute. Then repeat all six again. You can be as creative as you would like with the kind of exercise movements you choose. This equals to 12 minutes of exercise and should be done at least 3 times a week.

When you are Surge Training, you are elevating your heart rate and working it to its maximum. Oxygen is rapidly pumping through your body in larger amounts, which helps burn fat in higher quantities and more efficiently. Even when you are resting your body will continue to burn fat and build muscle.[305]

You will benefit the most from exercise when you keep your spinal cord and nerves in optimal shape. The nervous system is able to control millions of cells in dozens of body systems simultaneously. "While your body may be able to go

---

[304] Maximized Living, *"Surge Training Exercise Program,"* http://www.maximizedliving.com/5Essentials/MaximizedOxygenandLean Muscle/SurgeTrainingExerciseProgram.aspx [accessed August 1, 2011].

[305] Ibid.

days without water, weeks without food, and even minutes without oxygen, it cannot keep going one second without the power created by your nervous system!"[306]

Getting chiropractic adjustments from a doctor who focuses on overall health and longevity and who starts with correcting and maintaining your spine will allow for maximized nerve supply. You can realize great health benefits from good chiropractic care.

Looking back, I realized that I had habitually overloaded my schedule and then exercise became too difficult to fit into my daily routine. It was just one more thing to do! However, this was also frequently true about my time with God. So what was the real issue? What I found was a number of lies at the core of this "busyness". I began dealing with the lies I believed - lies such as "my performance determines my worth" or "I have to do well or be perfect to be loved" or "I have to be approved by certain others". As I exchanged these lies for God's truth, I found myself letting go of my need to be busy and my need to prove myself. I realized that I had taken on so many responsibilities that I had no time to be outdoors in nature and little time to be in activities with others.

As I began to experience inner healing, I began to drink in God's beauty in nature. As I found my time in nature connecting me with God, I discovered that walking, hiking, or biking was no longer a chore, but a blessed way of spending time with God in a place that spoke volumes about him and what he had created. The exercise was no longer the main objective; my time with God became the main event. I even began to ride my bike to work or to church at times, to walk places I had normally driven my car, to work in the garden, and to do yoga-type stretching as I listened to hymns and prayerful music. This felt less like the dread of exercise and more like the joy of loving God through what he had created!

---

[306]Maximized Living, *"Health Essential #2: Maximized Nerve Supply."* http://www.maximizedliving.com/HealthEssentials/ MaximizedNerveSupply.aspx [accessed August 1, 2011].

Could it be that you, too, are too busy to take care of yourself? Your stress level and emotions will be a red flag when you are doing too much work and not enough exercise and relaxation. You may want to consider how connected your emotional health is to your physical health in order to see how unresolved issues can make you more vulnerable to stress.

In addition, taking care of spiritual issues, such as unforgiveness, bitterness, an unsurrendered heart, and unconfessed sin can free you from some of the tension that may be in your daily lives. Also, taking a look at the lies that are wrapped around your life and exchanging them for God's Truth can have an amazing impact on your physical health and motivation to better care for yourself. (We will look at this aspect of your wholeness in the next part of this book.) This only points out how connected our bodies really are and how wholeness must infiltrate every part of our being.

Proper breathing

Maximized oxygen is essential for life. Most of us suffer from a lack of oxygen. Whether from improper breathing, poor diets, air pollution or lack of exercise, our cells are being deprived of this vital element and thus weakening our immune system.[307]

Proper breathing, along with exercise, can be helpful for receiving the oxygen your body needs. The stomach slightly protrudes and the rib cage expands when you breathe correctly. Since oxygen is needed for cell metabolism and respiration, as well as proper brain function, this natural rhythm of breathing becomes essential for one's physical health. "Proper breathing... increases lung capacity and energy levels, speeds the healing process of many disorders,

---

[307] Natural Cleansing Techniques, *"The Importance of Oxygen,"* http://www.naturalcleansingtechniques.com/oxygen.html [accessed August 1, 2011].

and helps to relieve anxiety, asthma symptoms, insomnia, and stress."[308] Babies breathe in a normal way, but under stress we sometimes lose this pattern of proper breathing and breathe rapidly and shallowly, creating hyperventilation or we breathe too slowly, creating hypoventilation. This can contribute to health problems, nervousness, and concentration difficulties. Since our mental and emotional state affects the way we breathe, proper breath management is an essential skill in stress management.

Try the following suggestions by Phyllis Balch when practicing deep and proper breathing:

- Slowly breathe in through your nose and from your abdomen as deeply as you can and hold the breath for a count of ten. Put your hand on your abdomen to make sure it is expanding as you breathe in. Place your tongue between your front teeth and the roof of your mouth. Slowly breathe out through your mouth. Do this for five minutes, three times daily.
- If you are under stress or need to relax quickly, place your arms down along the sides of your body. As you inhale deeply, stretch your arms up and out as if to form a V shape. Then exhale slowly through your mouth and bring your arms back down to your side. Repeat this as many times as you feel necessary.

Your lymph system functions by assisting the production of immune cells and relies on proper breathing and contraction of muscles to move the fluids of the lymph system around the body. You can facilitate this happening by regular exercise and deep breathing. You might want to try this Deep Breathing exercise several times a day:

- Empty your lungs by exhaling (pull in your stomach as you exhale)
- Take a deep breath in (your stomach expands)

---

[308] Ibid., 722.

114

- Hold your breath for twice as long as it took to breathe in
- Exhale for 4 times as long as it took to breathe it in
- Do this 8-10 times
- You will feel invigorated!

Obviously, an environment with fresh air, instead of an atmosphere with lots of traffic or pollution would be the best place for these exercises. Stale, polluted air can be as detrimental to your health as improper breathing.

Sabbath Rest

Sabbath comes from the Hebrew word *Shabbat*, which means to cease. A Sabbath rest is spoken about in a number of places throughout the Bible. The first time it appears is in the Creation story when it says, "God had finished the work he had been doing; so on the seventh day he rested from all his work."[309] By ceasing work, God establishes the "six days of work", the "one day of rest" pattern that is a healthy pattern for all of creation.

The first time God reminded the Israelites of this Sabbath principle was after their exit from Egypt when they were wandering in the wilderness. The people were to gather manna daily and only enough for each day. They quickly learned if they gathered more, it rotted and was full of maggots. But on the sixth day they were to gather enough for two days, since there would be no manna on the seventh day since it was to be a day of rest.[310]

Nevertheless, on the seventh day, some of the people went out to gather anyway but they didn't find anything. The Lord said to Moses, "How long will you refuse to keep my commands and my instructions? Bear in mind that the Lord has given you the Sabbath; that is why on the sixth day he

---

[309] Gen. 2:2-3

[310] Exod. 16:23

115

gives you bread for two days."[311] We begin to see the importance of this Sabbath principle when we observe the consequences that take place for those who fail to follow this principle in their lives.

God also reminded the Israelites of this principle in the Ten Commandments. "Remember the Sabbath day by keeping it holy...the seventh day is a Sabbath to the Lord your God."[312] On the Sabbath, ancient Israel set aside time for worship, prayer, and leisure.

But, this is not the only reason we are given the Sabbath command. God knew that it would be easier for us to "do" than to "be", so he called us to a once-a-week *fast* from the busyness of doing so we could take time to be and to become.

I once heard a story about a group of people who were being guided through a wilderness area by an Indian guide. When arising on the third day of the journey, the leader of the group announced to the guide that they were ready to begin the day's journey. The guide sat motionless, not responding to the man's words. So, the leader spoke his announcement again with the same response. Becoming impatient and frustrated with the delay, the leader vociferously declared for the third time that they must be on their way. The Indian guide carefully looked at the man and announced that he would not budge from his resting place until his soul caught up with his body. This guide was not responding to a legalistic principle of a certain day of the week, but to an innate awareness of the need for Sabbath. The Sabbath principle is a reminder that we need time set aside from the distractions of life to regain a connection with our own soul and with its creator.

In the Old Testament God also commanded the Israelites to give their land a Sabbath every seventh year – a year of rest

---

[311] Gen. 17:28-29

[312] Exod. 20:8

for their land.[313] He knew that even the earth needed time to rest after giving of itself for a period of time. In Heb. 4:9 the writer reminds us that the people of God also need a Sabbath-rest. "For anyone who enters God's rest also rests from his own work, just as God did from his. Let us, therefore, make every effort to enter that rest..." The Sabbath is not only an Old Testament command, but a wise principle for us.

However, not only is a time of Sabbath important on a weekly basis, but adequate rest is essential each night. The Psalmist reminds us that "It is useless for you to work so hard from early morning until late at night, anxiously working for food to eat; for God gives rest to his loved ones."[314]

Rest and adequate sleep will benefit not only our physical bodies, but our emotional health as well. Experts recommend getting between six to nine hours of sleep each night for optimum health and indicate that less than six can have negative health effects on us, even increasing our risk of dying[315]. There seems to be an extra benefit for going to bed before midnight. Experts tell us that one hour of sleep before midnight is equivalent to four hours afterward![316]

Consider these words of Ruth Haley Barton:

Lord, On the Sabbath,
body and soul reach out for time of a different sort,
time that is full of space rather than activity.
Time to watch the burning bush
in our own backyard...
the movement of the wind among bare branches...

---

[313] Lev. 25:5

[314] Ps. 127:2

[315] This advice came from http://www.aolhealth.com on June 30, 2008.

[316] Jordan Rubin, *The Maker's Diet* (Lake Mary, FL: Siloam, 2004).

the last leaf that clings to the branch
before its final letting go.

Letting go is hard,
letting go of that which no longer works...
That which no longer brings joy and meaning...
That which is no longer full of life...(and full of you)!

For many years, I violated some of the principles of physical health. I found out early in life that if you perform well and work circles around everyone else, you will get applauded. People would say to me at church, "I don't know how you get so much done"? This was music to a workaholic's ears! On top of that, I was a master caretaker. After all, wasn't that what the Bible taught us to do – love and give ourselves away to everyone else? I later learned that I could function this way only because I was a drug addict. Yes, it was a chemical called adrenaline and I didn't need a prescription for it because it was created within my own body and was available 24/7. I was so drawn to it because it elevated my mood and helped me have lots of energy to do many things. This busyness and ability to perform well helped block out my feelings of insignificance, inadequacy, insecurity, and my fear of rejection.

But, I was an accident waiting to happen! Since my focus was on everything and everyone else, I was not taking care of my own emotional well-being and physical health. And, when in 2002 I encountered the most challenging trial of my life, a marital crisis, I had no resources left. Thankfully, I was granted a short sabbatical that summer and my busyness came to an abrupt halt. However, even though my physical body stopped moving, my emotions and mind did not. What followed were some painful consequences that resulted from the withdrawal of my chemical addiction to adrenaline. I had a lot of generalized anxiety, could not sleep at night, lost weight, and felt like I was going to lose my mind. During the first month, my mind never slowed down – it raced constantly.

Nevertheless, I planned no schedule, made no appointments, and spent hours in silence and solitude - an interesting project for a woman who had never slowed down in her entire life! But, Jesus was right, "You're blessed when you're at the end of your rope. With less of you there is more of God and his rule."[317] I was about to learn how really connected our bodies are physically, emotionally, and spiritually. Several noteworthy things took place within the next several years.

First, I attended the twelve-step meeting of Al-Anon, in order to satisfy an assignment for my graduate program. I thought I was there for a class assignment, but after attending a few meetings, I wrote in my journal, "I feel like I have just looked straight into the face of myself!" Through Al-Anon I learned how codependency and enabling had contributed to the unhealthy physical overload of my life.

Second, I availed myself to some helpful resources. I went to counseling, attended a seminar on Inner Healing Prayer, and went on a weekend retreat called "the Healing of the Inner Child". I was introduced to some processes that helped heal my inner self, which allowed me to grow spiritually and emotionally. Through the retreat, I was connected with a Spiritual Director who spoke deeply into my life.

Third, a serendipitous connection, later realized as a God miracle, took place between two women and me during the fall of 2004. Connie, Norma and I had the privilege of studying the Bible together, becoming not only a support group for one another, but accountability partners. Their love and prayers supported me during a very difficult time, enabling me to grow in ways I had never grown before.

Fourth, I found out that I had osteoporosis, a loss of bone mass. This realization, along with its consequences, led me to commit my physical health to God. Wherein I had struggled

---

[317] Matt. 5:3 [MSG].

with exercise in the past, I began to enjoy walking in God's nature and doing yoga-type stretching.

All of this resulted in an amazing change in my life spiritually, physically, and emotionally! My health issues with candida, allergies, and digestion began to disappear and I no longer had a racing mind or a stressed schedule. I was no longer a workaholic or an adrenaline addict. Amazingly enough, these changes were the result of a continuous surrender to God, not the outcome of my own efforts.

In the past, I had tried to solve my health issues through books, nutrition, natural health, and doctor visits. I had fanatically practiced concepts I found in books on healthy living and self-help methodology, willingly embracing alternative methods of healing, and crazily controlling the things that went into my mouth. At one time, I had over a hundred books on health. I believed I could control my physical health by the things I did and didn't do - another legalistic and humanistic concept I had accepted.

But when I began to surrender my will to God, sit in his presence, bask in his love, meditate on his word, God began to change me in ways I never could have changed on my own. That was because God was in control now, not me. With his strength, I had become peaceful, God-centered, and balanced!

Gracious and loving God, you know the deep inner
patterns of my life that keep me from being totally yours.
You know the misformed structures of my being
that hold me in bondage to something less
than your high purpose for my life.
You also know my reluctance to let you have
your way with me in these areas.
Hear the deeper cry of my heart for wholeness
and by your grace enable me to be open
to your transforming presence.[318]
-Robert Mulholland

---

[318] Ibid., 19.

GOING DEEPER ⇩

Reflection Questions *(for Individuals or a Group)*

CONNECTING WITH GOD
Settle yourself into a comfortable sitting position. Breathe slowly and scan through your body, noticing any tightness. Then release any muscle that feels tight. When your body feels relaxed, sit in God's presence and connect with him. (Conclude this time with a short prayer.)

THINKING OUTLOUD

1. What is one thing you could change about your lifestyle that might have the greatest impact on your physical wholeness (eating habits, sleeping patterns, exercise, taking a Sabbath, etc.)?

2. How is what God thinks about these three things different from the way our culture views them?
   - Exercise
   - Food
   - Productivity, busyness, Sabbath rest

   (Prayerfully ask God to help you hear his voice about these issues instead of the voices of this culture.)

3. How much sugar would you say you ingest on a regular basis? (The average American consumes 170 pounds each year?) Are you aware of the amount of sugar in the foods you consume on a regular basis? *(Check out the sugar content of some of the food in your kitchen. Also, pay attention to the sugar content in foods you buy the next time you shop at the grocery)*

4. Consider renting one of the following DVDs and watching it yourself (or in a group): *Processed People*; *Fork Over Knives*; *Foodmatters*; or *Food, Inc.* How did this DVD challenge your

thoughts about eating? How do you think God feels about the food we put in our bodies? How can we honor him with the way we consume food?

BEING FORMED BY THE WORD
- Read I Cor. 3:16-17 in several versions. (If you have time, try doing a Lectio divina in Appendix B). Here's a couple you might want to read:
  o Do you not know that you are God's temple and that God's Spirit dwells in you? If anyone destroys God's temple, God will destroy him. For God's temple is *holy*, and you are that temple [ESV, italics added].
  o You realize, don't you, that you are the temple of God, and God himself is present in you? No one will get by with vandalizing God's temple, you can be sure of that. God's temple is sacred—and you, remember, are the temple [Message].
- Do you think this scripture applies to the way we care for our physical bodies? If so, how?
- Read John 2:13-17. Since we are now the *"temple of God"*, how might God feel when we bring things into it that harms it? [Compare that to Jesus' response in this passage.]
- Now that God lives within us, how does that change what we bring into the place where he resides?
- How can we decide what is God's way and what is the world's way concerning food, exercise, Sabbath, and sleep?

PRAYING FOR GOD'S HEART
- Read Robert Mulholland's prayer at the end of this section.
- Silently offer a prayer for what you are willing to let go of in order to embrace the physical wholeness God has for you.
- End by praying the Lord's Prayer together.

TAKING TIME TO BE FORMED

First Day:

If you find that you spend a considerable time engaged with media (TV, movies, video games, social media, surfing the internet, etc.) try going on a media fast. This will not only help starve the addiction and give you more time to exercise but will also limit some of the influence the media has on your eating habits. It takes 6-12 weeks to implement and master a healthy habit in your life. This fast can give you time to start some new habits that can nourish not only your physical wholeness but your emotional and spiritual wholeness as well!

Second Day:

If exercise is uninteresting to you, try incorporating a physical activity into your time with God - such as prayer walking or walking in nature as you memorize scripture. Or you might consider exercising with others - walking, hiking, or doing the 13" surge (an exercise method explained earlier). These ideas can be physically, spiritually, and socially refreshing without the usual dread that accompanies exercise.

• How did it feel when you tried one of these suggestions?

Third Day:

Completely changing your diet might seem overwhelming to you right now, but consider making several of these lifestyle choices:
• Reduce portion size at all meals by 20 percent
• Limit fast-food intake to only twice a month
• Drink more water daily (limiting soda and coffee)
• Indulge in junk food no more than once a week
• Replace junk foods with things, such as veggies, raw nuts or your favorite fruit, etc.

123

- Limit eating after a certain time at night, such as 2-3 hours before bedtime
- Consider asking someone else to do this with you (for accountability). How hard was this? How did it feel?

Fourth Day:

In silence reflect on where you are on the following scale:

Fully energized and refreshed	Good tired	Feeling tired and weary	Fully in a state of dangerous tired

If you find yourself toward the right side of the continuum, ask yourself the following questions:

- Have I been overly busy and rushing through life?
- Have I failed to honor the Sabbath principle of quiet and rest for my body and soul?
- Do I get enough sleep?
- Is my life out of balance?
- Could there be a lie or hurt that is driving my busy, exhausted lifestyle?

Read Matthew 11:28 slowly several times and sit quietly before the Lord, committing the situation to him. Listen in the quietness for what he wants to say to you.

Fifth Day:

If you try to change your eating, exercise, sleep, and Sabbath patterns only as sheer willpower, you will fail. It must be done because you love God and want to honor him with your habits and patterns. Spend time with God this week offering your physical habits to him out of your love for him. Read Eph. 3:16-21, I Cor. 16:13-14 and I Cor. 3:16-17.

Bibliography

Balch, Phyllis. *Prescription for Nutritional Healing,* 3rd Ed. N. Bergen, NJ: The Vitamin Shoppe, 2000.

Campbell, Colin, and Thomas Campbell. *The China Study: Startling Implications for Diet, Weight Loss and Long-term Health.* Dallas, TX: BenBella Books, 2006.

Food & Chemical Effects on Acid / Alkaline Body Chemical Balance, http://www.perque.com/ HSC_AcidAlkChart_7-07FINAL.pdf [accessed August 1, 2011]

Fuhrman, Joel. *Eat to Love.* Boston: Little Brown and Company, 2003.

Hardick, B.J., Kimberly Roberto, and Ben Lerner, *MaximizedLiving Nutrition Plans.* Celebration, FL: Maximized Living, 2009.

Jaffe, Russell. *"Food & Chemical Effects on Acid / Alkaline Body Chemical Balance,"* http://www.perque.com/ HSC_AcidAlkChart_7-07FINAL.pdf [accessed August 1, 2011].

Keehan, S. *"Health Spending Projections through 2017,"* Health Affairs Web Exclusive W146 (February 2008).

Maximized Living, *"Health Essentials,"* http://www.maximizedliving.com/NutritionDetox/ MaximizedQualityNutrition.aspx [accessed August 1, 2011].

McCasland, S.V. *The Interpreter's Dictionary of the Bible.* Nashville: Abingdon Press, 1962.

Mulholland, Robert. *Invitation to a Journey.* Downers Grove, IL: InterVarsity Press, 1993.

Natural Cleansing Techniques. *"The Importance of Oxygen,"* http://www.naturalcleansingtechniques.com/oxygen.ht ml [accessed August 1, 2011].

Newman, Deborah. *Comfortable in your own Skin: Making Peace with your Body Image.* Carol Stream, IL: Tyndale House Publishers, 2007.

Omartian, Stormie. *Greater Health God's Way.* Eugene, OR: Harvest House Publishers, 1996.

Oswald, Roy. *Clergy Self-Care.* Herndon, VA: Alban Institute, 1991.

Page, Linda Rector. *Healthy Healing,* 10th Ed. Healthy Healing Publishing, www.healthyhealing.com., 1997.

Pollan, Michael. *Food Rules: An Eater's Manual.* New York:Penguin Group, 2009.

Roberts, Elizabeth and Elias Amidon, eds. *Earth Prayers.* San Francisco: Harpers, 1991.

Rubin, Jordan. *The Maker's Diet.* Lake Mary, FL: Siloam, 2004.

Simmons, Geoffrey Simmons. *What Darwin Didn't Know.* Eugene, OR: Harvest House Publishers, 2004.

St. Augustine. *Confessions of St. Augustine: The Modern English Version.* Grand Rapids, MI: Revell, 2008.

Additional Resources

Balswick, Judith K. and Jack O. Balswick. *Authentic Human Sexuality: An Integrated Christian Approach.* Downers Grove, IL: InterVarsity Press, 1999.

Friberg, Nils C. and Mark R. Laaser. *Before the Fall: Preventing Pastoral Sexual Abuse.* Collegeville, MN: The Liturgical Press, 1998.

Grenz, Stanley J. *Betrayal of Trust: Sexual Misconduct in the Pastorate.* Downers Grove, IL: InterVarsity Press, 1995.

Grenz, Stanley J. *Sexual Ethics: An Evangelical Perspective.* Louisville, KY: Westminster John Knox Press, 1990.

Hazard, David. *Reducing Stress.* Eugene, OR: Harvest House Publishers, 2002.

Hutchcraft, Ron. *Living Peacefully in a Stressful World.* Grand Rapids, MI: Discovery House Publishers, 2000.

Joy, Donald M. *Bonding: Relationships in the Image of God.* Nappanee, IN: Evangel Publishing House, 1999.

Laaser, Mark R. *Healing the Wounds of Sexual Addiction.* Grand Rapids, MI: Zondervan, 2004.

Rubin, Jordan S. *Restoring your Digestive Health.* New York: Kensington Publishing, 2003.

Yancey, Philip. *Designer Sex.* Downers Grove, IL: InterVarsity Press, 2003.

DVD Resources

Eric Schlosser. 2008. *Food, Inc.* DVD. Directed by Robert
    Kenner. Los Angeles: Magnolia Home Entertainment.

Andrew Saul and Charlotte Gerson. 2009. *FoodMatters,* DVD.
    Directed by James Colquhoun and Laurentine ten
    Bosch. Metuchen, NJ: Passion River Films.

T. Colin Campbell. 2011. *Forks Over Knives,* DVD. New
    York: Virgil Films & Entertainment.

John Robbins, Joel Fuhrman, and Jeff Nelson. 2009.
    Processed People, DVD. Directed by Jeff Nelson.
    Porter Ranch, CA: Mostly Magic Media.

Part IV

HOLY AND WHOLE: In Soul

He makes me lie down in green pastures,
he leads me beside quiet waters, he restores my soul.
-Psalm 23:2-3

Whenever two people meet there are really six people present.
There is each man as he sees himself, each as the
other person sees him, and each man as he really is.
-William James

Our lack of emotional wholeness can hinder the progress we are able to make in other areas of our life. For instance, spiritual maturity cannot be achieved apart from an integration of the emotional aspects of who we are and without an intimate connection with God. On the other hand, unresolved emotional issues can thwart our efforts at maintaining a healthy and balanced diet or a consistent exercise program. It can also hinder or hurt our relationships with others.

Chapter 15

Boundaries

One of the first signs that can indicate problems in the area of emotional wholeness is problems in setting and enforcing boundaries in one's life. Healthy boundaries tend to be a serious concern for those actively involved in church activities. Such settings tend to reward codependent, counterproductive behaviors, encouraging the very conduct that is destructive to a follower of Christ. Often the person's need for affirmation or the underlying message that this is "God's work" creates an atmosphere where setting limits is difficult. They then fail to see the warning signs that indicate a need for personal growth.

Take a moment to check the statements that apply to you in the following self-test.

Boundaries Self-Test

o   I haven't taken a vacation in the last year
o   I haven't spent quality time with my family or friends lately
o   I am too busy to take a Sabbath (day of rest and restoration)
o   It's hard for me to say "No" to others
o   I have a hard time making decisions in life
o   I give often of myself to others, but hate to ask or allow
o   others to give to me
o   I tend to hurt others when trying to get my own needs met
o   I feel responsible for other people's happiness
o   I find I am highly competitive
o   When I am criticized, I either get defensive or I accept what they say as true and feel bad about myself
o   I often think about mistakes I've made and feel bad about myself
o   I will ignore my own personal rights or needs in order to please others

o   I allow others to define me
o   I expect others to anticipate my needs or to automatically
o   fill them
o   I feel afraid of God
o   I spend time looking at pornography
o   I was physically, sexually, verbally or emotionally abused as
    a child
o   I have been in several relationships where I have been
    physically or sexually abused (or made to feel worthless)

These statements indicate some possible concerns in the area of boundaries. Reread the statements that you checked as applicable to yourself. Consider talking to a counselor or trusted friend concerning issues of concern in your answers.

Persons with healthy boundaries are more likely to respond in these ways:

o   They are willing to say no when it is appropriate; they are
    also willing to say yes.
o   They have the ability to make requests and to seek
    alternatives when others say "no" to them.
o   They have a strong sense of identity and self-respect.
o   They make appropriate self-disclosure (includes revealing
    information about one's self) gradually and only as mutual
    sharing takes place and trust develops.
o   They expect shared responsibility in relationships.
o   They recognize when a problem is theirs or another
    person's. When it's not their problem, they don't take
    responsibility for it or try to rescue the other person.
o   They do not accept disrespect or abuse to themselves by
    other persons.

Boundaries are meant to define limits in our life. They identify not only where "I" end and "you" begin, but the space between us. They help us establish healthy relationships in which we understand who we are, how we should act, and how others should act toward us. They influence how we deal with the "self-in-relationship" dilemma which we call self-differentiation. Self-differentiation is the process of trying to balance being close and connected to others, while maintaining our own autonomy and self. Our minds accommodate these two conflicting needs by the making and unmaking of boundaries. In healthy differentiation we do not need to change the other person to meet our expectations, or change ourselves to meet the other's expectations.

Boundaries are generally established during our developmental years. Jane Adams contends that these mental structures increase in number and complexity as we experience other people and develop our own mental capacities. The bits and bytes of our mental process are formatted based on our memories, experiences, thoughts, emotions, sensations, associations, and impulses. This enables us in distinguishing our thoughts and feelings, our minds and emotions, from those of others. And while they occupy a territory of mental rather than physical geography, they're no less real than a wall, a fence, or a border.

Since these guidelines are generally established during childhood, they can be distorted and confused by boundary violations. Things, such as neglect, abuse, and lack of love, as well as overprotection, enmeshment, and over control can misinform us concerning healthy boundaries and limits. Trauma, fear, loss, or even repeated experiences of emotional trespass may thicken inner boundaries as we attempt to wall off our feelings from our thoughts.

Research has shown that boundaries influence not only relationships with others but also emotional balance, personal values, and cognitive abilities. Boundary distortion and confusion is symptomatic of problems with drugs, alcohol, food, sex, spending, relationships, and other substances or activities that are considered to be addictions. "When inner boundaries are too weak or too porous, the self is empty and famished, forever in search of someone or something to fill it up; when they are too solid and rigid, we can never let

133

ourselves be known, touched, or moved. And when they are distorted, so is the space where psychological growth takes place."

The way a parent emotionally responds to a child can also distort that child's boundaries and create future boundary issues. For instance, if one of a child's parents has shared intimate secrets with them, if one of a child's parents preferred their company to that of their spouse, if a child was favored by one of the parents, or if one of the parents was overly interested in the child's sexuality or body, there is a strong likelihood that that child will have a deeply rooted distortion in their emotional and spiritual boundaries. Persons with distorted boundary issues will tend to choose relationships with people according to the way they were treated or the way boundaries were modeled to them. They may feel they do not have a right to say no or to state what they will allow.

In relationships it is important that we maintain a balance between an ability to be close to an emotionally important other, while neither being dependent on gaining the other's acceptance and approval, nor fearing the other's disapproval, rejection or criticism. Inner growth and healing must take place in order for a person to reformat their beliefs about themselves as they learn to react with healthier boundary responses.

Boundaries are a key to how we deal with intimacy, loneliness, conflict, anxiety, stress, and challenge at every stage of life. We often find it much easier to set boundaries and assert ourselves in relationships that aren't as important to us; the real struggle takes place in relationships that mean the most to us. The reason this is true is because when we become emotionally invested in a relationship, our inner wounds from childhood tend to be most powerful and can be set off the easiest. We might be afraid that someone will cut us off, reject us, not approve of us, or get angry with us if we set a personal boundary and this can be threatening to our need for a relationship with them.

Boundary issues appear in basically three areas: physical, emotional, and spiritual. Physical boundaries define our body zone and may show up in the way we respond to physical touch, physical distance, and sexuality. Emotional boundaries define the protective safety zone around our feelings, self-esteem, and relationships and how we respond to the thoughts of others about ourselves. Spiritual boundaries define the territory around our relationship with God. Since we sustain both an intellectual and emotional understanding of God's love, grace, and affirmation, a sense of healthy spiritual boundaries are important to a vital personal relationship with God.

Boundaries can help define a number of things.

*   Each person's responsibility (Gal. 6:4-5)
*   The importance of protecting our hearts (Prov. 4:23)
*   Who we are to take responsibility for (Prov. 19:19)
*   Healthy limits for time management (Matt. 10:14)
*   How to respond to unhealthy people (Matt. 7:6)
*   Who to establish intimate relationships with (II Cor. 6:14)
*   What to avoid (I Thess. 4:3)

The Bible provides us with a number of good examples of boundary statements or actions.[319] As we grow in wholeness we begin to realize who we are, how we should act, and how others should behave toward us. This assists us in maintaining healthy boundaries which are essential to not only our ministries, but our spiritual, physical, and emotional well-being.

---

[319] Read Luke 4:42-44, Gen. 2:16-17, Exod. 20:1-17, Exod. 18:13-26, and James 5:12 for these examples.

Chapter 16

True Self, False Self

One of the key issues in emotional wholeness is the development of the self. The self that God fashioned is not a fixed-up, pretend self. God loves our actual self – the real us that he created in his image. But we tend to confuse our true self with some ideal self that we think we need to be for one reason or another.

The roots of our pretend self (or false self) lie in the childhood discovery that if we present ourselves in the way others want us to, we will receive love. This behavior is often reinforced by parents, teachers, and those in the church and community. Somewhere along the line, as this is repeatedly reinforced, we lose touch with our actual self.

A vast difference can be seen between the true self and false self. The false self seeks security and significance by what it HAS, what it DOES, and what others THINK of it. Thomas Merton describes this as "winding experiences around myself...like bandages in order to make myself perceptible to myself and to the world, as if I were an invisible body that could only become visible when something visible covered its surface."[320] The false self finds its identity in the self it wants others to think it is. This identity is achieved by means of pretense and practice and is maintained by control and by its own efforts.

A visual picture of the risks of the false self can be seen in the following story of the baby crab. The baby crab has an irresistible temptation for discarded bottles that lay on the ocean floor.

---

[320] Thomas Merton, *New seeds of contemplation* (New York: New Directions, 1961).

The little creature...glides easily through the bottle's mouth to discover an enclosed world that offers everything it needs: plenty of organic debris to eat, shelter from strong currents, and, best of all, protection from the countless predators who feed on young crabs. Delighted, it makes itself at home, and begins to thrive in the cozy surroundings. After some weeks, however, when instinct tells it the time has come to migrate, it crawls confidently to the opening, expecting to swim back out the way it came in. That's when it discovers the ghastly price of that time of perfect security: it's grown too big to fit through the neck of the bottle! In a terrible ironic twist that (seemingly) safe shelter now becomes a death chamber; its protective shield will be its coffin.[321]

The life of the false self is formed around the desire for protection, too. It surrounds itself with excessive attachments, which may include possessions, accomplishments, dreams, memories, or relationships. All of these are blessings when held in open hands of gratitude, but become curses when grasped in clenched fists of entitlement and viewed as belonging to us.

On the other hand, the true self seeks security and significance by being deeply loved by God. Its fulfillment is found in an unthinkable way - in surrender to God. It bases its identity in "who it is" and "who it is becoming" *in Christ*. It is maintained by grace instead of by its own efforts and mirrors the love-image of God.

Franciscan priest Richard Rohr maintains that there is no more challenging spiritual issue than the problem of the self. He believes that most of contemporary spiritual teaching is still trying to inspire and fortify the private self, the

---

[321] Talbert Holtz, *Street wisdom: Connecting with God in everyday life* (Mystic, CT: Twenty-Third Publications, 2003), 1.

autonomous "I." That may be one of the reasons we struggle with forming authentic community in the church today. Much of the church's efforts are spent trying to evangelize and sacramentalize what many would call the false self. The church has not been as concerned about transformation as they have been about beliefs, practices or loyal membership. Because of this, both the individual and society remain largely unchanged. Peter K. Gerlach, MSW[322] gives us these helpful comparisons between the true self and false self:

Common TRUE SELF Traits	Common FALSE SELF Traits
Alert, awake, aware	Distracted, confused, numb
Mood is generally up and light	Often heavy, down and gloomy
Usually realistically optimistic	Usually pessimistic or idealistic
Focused, clear, and centered	Confused, vague, unfocused
Compassionate, forgiving	Blaming, critical
Firm, strong, motivated, purposeful	Indecisive, anxious, unsure, cautious
Calm, serene, peaceful, at stillness of heart	Upset, scared, angry, guilty, ashamed
Usually has a wide-angle, long-range focus – accepts delayed gratification	Usually has a narrow, short-term focus – delayed gratification is hard
Balances long and short-term payoffs	Usually seeks immediate gratification
Usually patient, persistent, committed	Often impatient, impulsive, uncommitted
Appreciative, grateful, "glass-half-full"	Bitter, jealous, resentful, glass "half-empty"
Empathic, sensitive, genuinely respectful	Selfish, arrogant, disrespectful

[322] Peter K. Gerlach, "Who Runs Your Life?" Break the Cycle, http://sfhelp.org/01/f+t_selves.htm [accessed August 9, 2008].

Spiritually open, aware, "connected," receptive, growing	Spiritually unaware, skeptical, closed, scornful, or uninterested
Consistently self-nurturing without egotism	Consistently neglects one's self
Genuine, honest, open, direct	Dishonest, indirect, controlling
Respectfully assertive	Timid, apologetic or aggressive
Socially engaged and active	Isolated or compulsively social
Able to form genuine bonds with others	Difficulty forming true (vs. pseudo) bonds
Spontaneously expressive of *all* emotions, without major anxiety or guilt	Anxious, guilty, or blocked about feelings or expressing some or all emotions
Able to judge who to trust with what and when to not trust	Difficulty discerning who to trust with what
Realistically self-responsible	Notably over- or under-responsible
Usually realistic about life and situations	Frequent distortions and denials
Spontaneously able to both give and receive love	Difficulty giving and/or receiving *real* love
Comfortable receiving merited praise	Uncomfortable receiving merited praise
Often able to forgive self and others	Difficulty forgiving self and/or others
Frequently includes others in their focus and awareness	Often focuses only on themselves
Seldom gives double messages	Often gives double messages
Able to grieve losses	Difficulty grieving losses
Seeks self-guided people and high-nurturance settings	Unconsciously prefers wounded people and low-nurturance settings
Living a clear life-purpose	Unclear to a life purpose
Physically healthy: balanced diet, exercise, work and rest balanced; preventive checkups	Physically unhealthy: relies on prescribed or self-medication; work, play, and rest unbalanced

The false self can become deeply entrenched in a person's life. You can change your name, address, religion, job, and outward appearance, but if you do not allow the false self to die and the true self, created by God, to resurface, the false self will simply adjust to the new environment. If we are going to penetrate our delusions, we must have a relentless commitment to truth and a deep sense of freedom from the fear of rejection. The true self can exist only in relation to God and its clearest expression can be seen in the life of Jesus who lived his whole life consistently in relationship with God.

Since Jesus was both fully man and fully God, he too had to battle with the temptation to put on the false self. When Jesus was led into the desert[323] he was tempted by Satan to establish his identity on his doing,[324] on prestige,[325] and on what he possessed.[326] Thankfully, Jesus knew who he was in God and could resist the temptation to live out of a false self based on these things. Instead he grounded his identity in a relationship with the Father and lived out his calling embracing his true self and living in submission to God, even death on the cross. Jesus informs us that in order to be his disciple we must deny ourselves and take up his cross and follow him.[327] (Matt. 16:24). A part of this cross involves letting our false self die in order that our true self can emerge. A purely individual approach to our true self will be inadequate to accomplish this. It will call for a strong connection with God and a healthy connection with others.

Every moment of every day God comes into our inner garden seeking companion-ship with us. But he finds us

---

[323] Matt. 4:1-11

[324] Matt. 4:3

[325] Matt. 4:5-6

[326] Matt. 4:8-9

[327] Matt. 16:24

141

hiding in the bushes of our false self. Coming out of hiding requires that we embrace the vulnerabilities that originally sent us into hiding. So the first step back toward our true self is a step toward honesty. You may want to try these things, suggested by David Benner[328], as you move toward becoming your true self:

1. Ask God to help you see what makes you feel most vulnerable, causing you to run and hide. It could be conflict, failure, pain, fear, childhood wounds, emotional upset, or loss. Then step out and allow God to embrace you and your vulnerability.

2. Which image of your "self" are you most attached? Ask God to help you see the ways you defend yourself against vulnerability. Then ask for his help in letting go of these.

3. Spend time concentrating on "who you are in Christ", based on the truths of God's Word. Sit in his presence, allowing him to love you and affirm your worth that is based in him.

4. Slowly you will be able to let go of the need to base your "self" on what you have, what you do, and what others think of you.

Familiarize yourself with the traits of the "true self" (in the chart above) and when you notice that a vulnerability has caused you to retreat back into your false self, quiet yourself in God's presence and center your attention on him. As you focus on him and your identity in him, you will return to a peaceful place where your true self can again surface and blossom.

---

[328] David Benner, *The gift of being yourself* (Downers Grove, IL: InterVarsity Press, 2004).

Chapter 17

Thoughts and Emotions

In order to grow in the area of emotional growth, we will begin by looking at the importance of a connection between our thoughts and our emotions. A healthy emotional life will involve a strong connection between the two. We can find a helpful example of this in the life of Jesus. He was able to stay connected with his logical thinking while expressing his feelings and emotions. Let us take a look at some examples of this.

The first example concerns the death of his friend, Lazarus. When Jesus sees Mary, as well as the Jews who had come with her, weeping regarding Lazarus' death, he is deeply moved in spirit and troubled. The New Revised Standard Version uses the words, "greatly disturbed in spirit and deeply moved;" whereby the New Living Translation says he is angry and deeply troubled.[329]

The passage goes on to say that when they invite him to "come and see"; he weeps.[330] These emotions do not indicate just a slight feeling, but point to deep emotions that lead him to an expression of tears. Jesus connects with his feelings, but he does not get stuck in them. He goes to the grave, speaks to Martha about "believing", prays to his father concerning the situation and then calls Lazarus forth. His emotions are not isolated from his rational thinking capacity. They are connected and he moves easily from one to another.

The second example takes place as Jesus approaches Jerusalem. In Luke 19:41 we are told that "as he approached Jerusalem and saw the city, he wept over it". The Jews have failed to see him as the Messiah and as their source of peace,

---

[329] Jn. 11:33

[330] Jn. 11:35

and he is moved to a deep expression of emotion as a response to this situation. We realize some of the reason for his deep emotions as we think back to his earlier words in Luke 13:34, "Jerusalem, Jerusalem, the city that kills the prophets and stones those who are sent to it! How often have I desired to gather your children together as a hen gathers her brood under her wings and you were not willing? We see Jesus being able to embrace both frustration and compassion at the same time. He is not blinded by his anger; he is in full control of his emotional response.

The third example takes place soon after he approaches Jerusalem. He enters the temple in Jerusalem, sees the misuse of his Father's house and expresses his God-given feelings of emotion by driving out the money changers and merchants who are practicing dishonest and greedy business exploits.[331] We know he is angry because he even overturns the tables and the benches in the temple.[332] His earlier emotions of sadness, frustration, and compassion[333] culminate in the expression of anger as he dispenses consequences to these merchants for this injustice. This is actually the second time Jesus clears the temple, his anger also clearly evident in an account recorded in John 2:13-17. It is important to realize that Jesus was still in control of himself, for he immediately carries on a rational conversation with the Jews as they question his authority for these actions.[334] In this example we see the difference between uncontrolled rage and righteous indignation.

Jesus also expresses his emotions in the Garden of Gethsemane.[335] He is facing his own death by the painful

---

[331] Luke 19:45

[332] Matt. 21:12-16

[333] Luke 13:34

[334] Jn. 2:18-21

[335] Matt. 26:36-46; Mark 14:32-42; Luke 22:39-46

process of crucifixion and is troubled, deeply distressed, and overwhelmed with sorrow. Luke 22:44 indicates that his emotional response is so intense that his sweat is like drops of blood. Jesus is totally in touch with his emotions, but his feelings are still fully connected with his thought process for he is able to make a conscious decision of his will. His acceptance of the suffering, in accordance with God's plan, is apparent in these words, "My Father, if it is possible, may this cup be taken from me. Yet not my will but yours be done."[336]

Jesus was able to express his emotion with unashamed, unembarrassed freedom in all of these instances. There are a number of others occasions where Jesus expresses emotion: anger;[337] joy;[338] empathy/sorrow;[339] distress;[340] and astonishment/amazement.[341] As we reflect on all of these examples, we realize that a balanced personality involves the ability to both think our thoughts and feel our emotions in conjunction with one another. We can better understand this concept as we note what studies have revealed about the brain.

Neurologists have found that our thinking, feeling, and acting functions are designed to be in connection, in a three-tiered manner in the brain. In his book, *How your Church Family Works,* Peter Steinke describes the roles of each part.[342] The first tier is the base of the brain and tends to be reactive. It operates as an automatic process and is an

---

[336] Luke 22:42

[337] Mark 3:5

[338] Luke 10:21

[339] Luke 7:13

[340] Luke 12:50

[341] Mark 6:6, Luke 7:9

[342] Peter Steinke, *How Your Church Family Works* (Washington, DC: Alban Institute, 1993).

instinctive reaction, typical of not only functions such as breathing, but by also knee-jerk responses triggered by our emotions. The second tier is the limbic system and it controls our emotional responses. It is meant to play a mediating role between our emotional extremes, but under certain circumstances it goes haywire. These two sections of the brain compose only 15% of the brain mass, have easy access to one another, and include our involuntary responses.

On the other hand, an unbelievable 85% of the brain is made up of the cerebral hemisphere, which deals with our logical processes. This section has few connectors to the other two tiers, which means when we are full of emotions, it shuts down. That, in turn, can cause a disconnection between our thoughts and emotions which can result in a person reacting to a strong emotion without the support of their thinking process. How many times have you heard of someone making a drastic response to a situation when they were highly emotional?

Even Paul struggled with his own responses. He said, "I do not understand what I do. For what I want to do I do not do, but what I hate I do...I know that nothing good lives in me, that is, in my sinful nature. For I have the desire to do what is good, but I cannot carry it out."[343]

Often the thinking and feeling parts lose their normal connection because of a hurt or a trauma that has been experienced. The Greek word for trauma means "wound". It has been said that when a trauma takes place in someone's life, if they do not have post-trauma counseling or help in expressing their thoughts *and* feelings, the connectors between the emotional and cognitive will be disconnected from one another. This disassociation or separation of elements from one another initially helps reduce the impact of that particular experience, providing some protection at the time to the emotional system.

However, this is not meant to be a permanent solution because it can have lifelong consequences to our personal

---

[343] Rom. 7:15, 18

wholeness if the linkage remains disconnected. When future triggers occur or a similar type situation takes place, our tendency will be to react to this new situation by using only our logical thinking or only an emotional reaction. Sometimes our response makes no logical sense because we are caught up in our emotions. Or we respond in an unemotional analytical way because we lack access to our emotions.

Take for example a woman who is raped by a stranger. If she is not able to talk about the details of the rape and her feelings concerning it, she will likely have an unfortunate response to any new stimuli that she encounters. Say, for instance, when she is shopping in a mall she smells the cologne that her rapist wore. Her response is to frantically leave the mall because she is sure that her rapist is there. Since her emotions are isolated from her logical ability, she is unable to reason that other men may also wear that same cologne. She is restricted by her sensory and emotional memories of the rape and will be controlled by any triggers that recall it.

Let us now look at how this type of disconnection, between thoughts and emotions, can have a lifelong affect on us. At five years of age, Dolores and her mother are in a car accident. This proves to be the hazardous event that starts a chain reaction of happenings that will significantly affect her life. Dolores is basically unharmed, but her mother is seriously injured and subsequently hospitalized for a number of months. It takes a year for her mother to return to the normal activities in the home.

Her father is unavailable as well for a period of time after this - preoccupied with her mother's care and with his own emotions, having lost his own mother at the age of three. Six months after the accident Dolores experiences the sudden death of her Grandpa who is very special in her life. To add to her hurt her grieving grandma shuts her out, favoring her older sister, leaving her rejected now that Grandpa is gone.

Dolores is wounded by this series of events. She responds to this hurt by avoiding her emotions and functioning primarily out of her thought processes. She superimposes her feelings of abandonment upon multiple other situations that take place throughout her life. When someone is absent or unavailable for her, it triggers some of the same feelings of rejection she felt as a child, creating fresh pain within her. It takes many years and a lot of additional pain before Dolores is able to process this original hurt and reconnect her thoughts and feelings. Today, because of inner healing and an acceptance of God's love, Dolores is able to connect healthy emotions with God's truth. This has made an unbelievable difference in her life and in her relationships. I know... because I am Dolores.

Not only can this disconnect occur as a result of unfortunate life circumstances, such as in the case of Dolores, but as a result of any perceived trauma or hurt that occurs throughout a person's life. This includes abuse in any form – emotional, physical, sexual, and verbal. Satan loves to use trauma-type experiences in our life because trauma changes all the proper functioning of the brain. It wounds the brain, deregulates the body and brain chemistry, and causes an emotional and cognitive concussion. Those who have studied the brain report that trauma causes the left and right side of the brain to become disconnected from one another. This results in a traumatized person either having vivid, graphic thoughts with no emotions or intense emotions without rational thoughts or actual memories.[344]

---

[344] Norman Wright, *The New Guide to Crisis & Trauma Counseling* (Ventura, CA: Regal Books, 2003).

Chapter 18

Inner Healing of the Soul

We often try in our own strength to deal with our life stressors or our responses to them. But this never gets to the real issue. The symptoms may be different but the core issue is the same: we are trying to find a solution or get our worth and satisfaction in a way other than God.[345] Most people simply try to change their behavior without allowing the power of the Holy Spirit to heal and transform them. They are saved, but not free.

The following list, suggested by Wardle, outlines what is really taking place when we try to deal with the stress of life situations.[346]

> ➤ Life Situation (or stressor)
> ➤ Dysfunctional behavior
> ➤ Emotional Upheaval (fear, shame, guilt, anger)
> ➤ Lies & Distortion
> ➤ Wounds

First, there is a *frustrating situation or stressor* that takes place in our life. Stressful situations are common to us all and are a part of normal living. But how we choose to deal with them is the real issue.

There are a number of ways to deal with a stressful life situation: (1) Turn to God and trust Him; (2) Turn to other people as our resource; or (3) Respond in a way that we have

---

[345] Isa. 28:15; Psa. 107:9, 145:14-16

[346] Terry Wardle, *Healing Care, Healing Prayer: Helping the Broken Find Wholeness in Christ* (Abilene, TX: Leafwood Publishers, 2001).

in the past (*dysfunctional behavior, addiction,* our usual coping mechanisms, etc.).

If we find ourselves responding by repeating a certain habit or addictive behavior, it is generally because we have experienced a *powerful emotional feeling* that we cannot handle alone (fear, shame, guilt, anger, rejection, insecurity, worthlessness, hopelessness, etc.).

We often find that people will try to deal with their emotional upheaval or chaotic life by working on self-worth issues or stopping their behavior. Most 12 Step programs focus on recovery from the addictive behaviors. Some churches are focused mainly on getting rid of sin. But this is only dealing with the issues on the surface. There is much more underneath that is triggering our emotional response.

Feelings and emotions are not independent parts of our being that fire off at will. They are triggered by something we have believed about ourselves based on an experience we had as a child. And this childhood belief is usually not based on truth, but is a *"Lie of the enemy"* that attacks the way we think about ourselves and is in contrast to how God sees us. Here are some such lies: People always reject me, I am not worth loving, I cannot change, I must please other people, if I fail I am unworthy of love, and how well I do determines my worth.

In addition, under the lie is a wound. The lie was formed or believed because of a *wound or hurt* that took place in childhood. Since these hurts are painful, they create turmoil within us and often cause us to hide, put on a mask, withdraw, isolate, or run from the pain.

Wardle[347] suggests we address this situation by starting with the wounds, which are the real reason for our reaction.

➢ Healing of Wounds
➢ Replace Lies with Truth
➢ Experience peace

---

[347] Ibid.

- Empowered Living
- New response to Life Situations

We must begin by grieving and allowing the *wound to be healed*. This healing takes place through the power of the Holy Spirit.

The *lies are exposed and replaced with God's truth*. We begin identifying dysfunctional behavior (or our previous ways of coping) and address them not by renouncing them, but by surrendering them to God, spending time developing a close relationship with God and by accountability with a trusted person.

Now when we have emotional upheaval, we cope with it by turning to Christ. *Peace* is now what we experience.

We are *empowered* through the presence and power of the Holy Spirit who guides and directs our steps.

Then when *life situations* take place, we turn to God, instead of practiced habits and addictions, and he gives us strength to cope, unconditional love that satisfies and a peace that is based upon an absolute trust in Him.

Chapter 19

Lies and Truth

In his book, "Waking the Dead", John Eldredge says,

Most of us simply try to 'put things behind us,' get past it, forget the pain as quickly as we can. Really - denial is a favorite method of coping for many Christians. But not with Jesus. He wants truth in our inward being, and to get it there he's got to *take us into* our inmost being.[348]

While in the heart, he will uncover the lies buried down there, and bring in the truth that will set you free. Don't just bury it quickly; ask God what he wants to speak to.

Did you know that people, who train to recognize counterfeit money, do not study counterfeit money; they study real money? Therefore, one way we can get better at recognizing the lies is to know God's Truth – in other words the truth and the "real things". There is no shortcut for this step. This seed may take time to grow and may be hard work, but is worth it!

One great way to do this is to memorize bible scriptures. I know it sounds boring, but think of it as a way to prepare for battle. I have found it to be one of the most effective ways for me to have victory over Satan in my life. You can even pray God's word. If you are having difficulty overcoming a specific struggle in your life, I'd recommend trying it!

Beginning to recognize and uproot the weeds or lies in your life is your first step in learning how to gain self esteem. Often times those thoughts that keep coming up in your mind again and again (and tear you down instead of build you up)

---

[348]John Eldredge, *Waking the Dead: The Glory of a Heart Fully Alive* (Nashville: Nelson Books, 2003), 122.

will be those lies. I have heard this often called..."Stinkin' Thinkin"! Generally when you become aware of a wound in your life, you will also find a lie of the enemy attached to it. Lies and wounds tend to keep us stuck in destructive ways of thinking, in unhealthy ways of coping, and deprived of the love and freedom of Christ. Lies always originate from the enemy, not God.

A lie can be defined as an untrue statement made with the intent to deceive. That is always Satan's intent for "He was a murderer from the beginning, not holding to the truth, for there is no truth in him. When he lies he speaks his native language for he is a liar and the father of lies" (John 8:44). His lies are wrapped around a number of schemes that he uses to entrap our thoughts and emotions: secrecy (secrets have power), shame (feelings that we are flawed and worthless), deception (trickery), and distortion (to twist out of meaning).

Here is a list of some common lies that people might believe. Which of these lies have you believed at some point in your life? Which ones are you vulnerable to right now?

- I must be accepted by certain people in order to feel good about myself
- My unhappiness is someone else's fault
- My worth is dependent on how well I do – love must be earned
- Life should be fair
- I need to be perfect
- If I make a mistake, it means *I am* a failure
- You can and should meet my needs
- If anything goes wrong, it must be my fault
- I cannot change
- I cannot help the way I am
- People will not like me
- I should always be happy
- Christians will never have serious problems
- Anger is always wrong

154

- Godly Christians should never be depressed
- I will be rejected by people when they really get to know me
- I must be in control of certain situations
- It is my Christian duty to meet other people's needs
- I need other people to love me so I feel worthwhile
- I am not lovable or worth loving
- Physical beauty matters more than inner beauty
- I should not have to live with unfulfilled longings
- If I fail I am unworthy of love
- I cannot be happy unless I have the love and acceptance of certain people
- My outward appearance determines my worth
- I am a victim – bad things always happen to me
- I am a loser
- I cannot do anything right
- God doesn't love me
- God is not really enough
- God should fix my problems
- God is just like my father
- God cannot forgive what I have done
- I cannot walk in consistent victory over sin
- I should not have to suffer
- People let you down (disappoint you)
- My circumstances will never change
- If my circumstances were different, I would be happy

Robert McGee places Satan's lies in four distinctive categories[349]. I have added the fifth category.

---

[349] Robert McGee, *The search for significance* (Nashville: Word Publishing, 1998).

1. Performance Trap – I must meet certain standards to feel good about myself *(A person caught up in this lie may have a tendency toward workaholism, competitiveness, perfectionism, or a strong need to succeed)*

2. People Pleasing – I must be approved (accepted) by certain others to feel good about myself *(A person trapped in this lie may be vulnerable to fear of rejection, poor boundaries, codependency, lack of self-care or fear of being alone)*

3. Fear of Failure – Those who fail are unworthy of love and deserve to be blamed and condemned *(A person trapped in this lie may be vulnerable to feelings of insignificance and disappointment. They may also lack initiative, have difficulty making decisions and be overly self-critical.)*

4. Flawed and Defective – I am what I am; I cannot change. *(A person caught up in this lie may have feelings of shame, debasement, worthlessness and hopelessness.)*

5. Image/Possessions Trap – I am what I have.[350] *(A person trapped in this lie may have a tendency toward overspending (compulsive buying) or body image obsession since appearance and possessions are important in forming their worth and image.)*

Paul reminds us to watch that we are not taken *"captive* through...*empty deception*...according to the elementary principles of the world, rather than according to

---

[350] This is a category of lies that I have added. It is not included in McGee's book.

156

Christ".[351] The word captive comes from the Greek word *sulagogeo* and means "to carry off as a captive" or "to lead away from the truth". Other translations use the words, "enslave you" (GNT), "make a prey of you" (RSV), or captures you (NIRV). What better way can we find to describe the tactics of Satan?

The word for deception used here is *ajpavth* meaning deceit and deceitfulness. Additional meaning can be gained from the synonyms of this word: dishonesty, treachery, trickery, pretense, duplicity, falseness, and fraud. The translation of this Greek word *ajpavtha* is "apate" which comes close to our word "apostate" (defector, backslider) or "apostasy" (desertion, renunciation). The deception of the enemy should not be taken lightly for it is dangerous and has caused many people to walk away from the faith. It's not only "empty" deception (NAS), but also hollow (TNIV), worthless (GNT), false reasoning (NIRV), and not from Christ. This deception can take place not only through human beings or religious beliefs, such as was the case with the Gnostic beliefs that the Colossians were being exposed to, but also through the "ruling spirits of this world" (NCV) or "the spiritual forces of this world" (TNIV) which includes Satan, the prince of this world.[352]

I, too, got caught up in a number of lies of the enemy. As a child I longed for my daddy's love. My daddy worked so hard that he had little time to pay attention to me. As a preschooler a lie had begun forming around this desire, "I need my daddy to love me in order to feel worthwhile." Because of this desire, I began to pay close attention to how my daddy responded to me in order to see if I had his approval and love.

Around the age of five two incidents took place in my life that had a huge effect on me. First, my mother and I were in

---

[351] Col. 2:8 [NAB, italics added].

[352] John 12:31, Eph. 2:2

an unfortunate accident. The car we were traveling in spun in gravel and headed toward the river that ran parallel to the road. Fortunately we were saved from drowning by a tree we crashed into, but the tree hit on my mother's side of the car. My mother was penned into the car, bleeding profusely and was seriously injured. I was barely hurt but at the age of five I had no clue where to get help for us. Through a miracle of God, a nearby farmer found us and called for help. In the beginning they thought she would die from blood loss, but my mother miraculously survived. However, she spent several months in the hospital and the rest of the year recuperating.

My father was deeply affected by this incident, having lost his own mother at the age of three through death from influenza. Shortly after his mother's death, his own father abandoned him in order to chase after a woman that he believed he loved and needed. Why had his own father allowed him to go to an orphanage instead of keeping him? Why wasn't he a priority in his father's life? A generational lie was birthed in my father at the time of his mother's death and was reinforced by many circumstances that transpired throughout his unpredictable childhood.

Now this wound in my father's life was reopened by my mother's serious accident. Instead of dealing with it, my father ran from the painful memory by staying busy working all the time. To my childhood heart it felt like he had abandoned me too, just like his father had abandoned him. Why wouldn't he spend time with me? Why was he so angry and critical when I was in his presence? Didn't he love me?

A second incident took place shortly after the accident. During the first five years of life I became known as grandpa's girl and received special attention and love from him. But approximately four months after my mom's accident, my grandpa died suddenly from a massive heart attack. I again felt abandoned by an important person in my life. In addition I was also rejected by my grandma because every time she looked at me I reminded her of her own loss. How would I ever get love when those close to me kept abandoning me?

As time passed I started noticing that I could get words of approval from my dad if I did well - made good grades, played the piano well, and did what I was asked to do at home. A new lie was beginning to take shape in my life, "My worth is dependent on what I do and how well I do it." In other words, "love must be earned". Once this lie took root I fervently attempted to earn my father's love by what I did. But I needed to be perfect for if I failed, I might not receive the love I so desperately wanted and needed from him.

These lies followed me into adulthood as they developed deeper and deeper roots. With my love tank nearly on empty, I found myself always searching for the next way to get some love and approval – college degrees, being a good mother, a good pastor's wife, doing good things for others, and working day and night at the church. Unconsciously I was staying busy in order to block out my fear of abandonment and to suppress a new lie - I wasn't worth loving. I got so tangled up in these lies that I began wearing masks, avoiding real intimacy in relationships, and even avoiding a close relationship with God. I found myself trying to cope with my hurt with things such as: control, pride, perfectionism, manipulation, idle chatter, and constant busyness. I tried many different ways to fix this brokenness in my life, but I couldn't do it.

It took a serious trial in my life to provide the motivation for me to look deeply into myself. God began helping me exchange those lies in my life for his truth, one day at a time. He also began healing the wounds that were controlling my life. I was experiencing the fulfillment of God's promise that by *his* wounds we are healed.[353] The New Living Translation states it this way, "He was beaten so we could be whole. He was whipped so we could be healed."

Most of us are unaware of how thoroughly Satan can deceive us with his lies. However, we are not the only ones; the deception began from the very beginning with Adam and Eve when they were taken in by the schemes of the enemy.

---

[353] Isa. 53:5

159

In the third chapter of Genesis we find the account of this crafty serpent. Eve is not aware of who she is dealing with because the serpent has disguised himself as an angel of light.[354] He begins by putting doubt in Eve's mind about the command God gave them which said, "you must not eat from the tree of the knowledge of good and evil, for when you eat of it you will surely die".[355] His question, "Did God really say, 'you must not eat from any tree in the garden'"[356] is an attempt to not only put doubt in Eve's mind, but to confuse her about what God has said. In addition, he is attempting to distort the prohibition that God gave which was limited to only the tree of the knowledge of good and evil.

When Eve responds she embellishes what God has said, stating, "We may eat fruit from the trees in the garden, but God did say, 'you must not eat fruit from the tree that is in the middle of the garden, and *you must not touch it*, or you will die.'"[357] Eve first makes herself vulnerable to the Enemy by deliberating with him about what God has said, then secondly, by adding to what God really did say. By declaring that God was not even allowing her to "touch it", we note that she is starting to consider the idea that God might be unfair or unreasonable. What are the first thoughts or feelings you generally have when you are told you are not to touch something?

Satan sees an opening to deceive and begins the temptation, "You will not surely die *(an obvious contradiction to God's instructions)*....For God knows that when you eat of it your eyes will be opened and you will be like God."[358] Satan

---

[354] II Cor. 11:14

[355] Gen. 2:16-17

[356] Gen. 3:1

[357] Gen. 3:2-3 [italics added].

[358] Gen. 3:4-5

appeals to Eve's pride and to her desire to be like God. Satan knows the power of this appeal all too well, for he succumbed to the same temptation himself.[359] However, the desire to be like God was not the real problem, for God had created them in the Divine image and wanted them to be like him. "The core of the lie that Adam and Eve believed was that they could be like God *without God*. But without God the most we can ever do is make ourselves into a god".[360]

He is also putting doubt in her mind about God's motives - maybe God isn't going to give her everything she needs or wants. Could God be keeping something from her? Once Eve accepted these assumptions, her desire for the fruit grew. She sees that it is "good for food, pleasing to the eye, and also desirable for gaining wisdom",[361] so she takes some, eats it, and then offers it to Adam. The result is life altering consequences for both of them.

When we begin to doubt whether we can completely trust God, Satan has the opportunity to ensnare us in a lie that will move us away from spiritual and emotional wholeness. Hurts and childhood wounds can cause us to doubt whether God really loved us enough to protect us from these situations or to keep them from happening to us. A seed of uncertainty is then planted within us about God's trustworthiness and often results in us choosing to find our own ways to meet our needs. We begin thinking, "If God will not help and protect me, I will have to do it myself".

Remember, the Enemy knows where there are still gaping, open wounds in our life. He will seek to get us back in touch, over and over again, with the hurt we felt, so we will fall for the lie and deception he is trying to use. Unless there is a

---

[359]I John 3:8, Rev. 12:7-9

[360] David Benner, *The Gift of Being Yourself* (Downers Grove, IL: InterVarsity Press, 2004), 79.

[361] Gen. 3:6

process of healing for these wounds, we are vulnerable to the tactics of Satan.

Healing begins when we are open and honest about our wounds with a safe person, and seek to find healing and restoration. Healing involves the recognition of lies we have believed and a process for replacing those lies with God's truth. We can then protect what Satan might try to use. Robert McGee maintains that we have "reached a true mark of maturity when we begin testing the deceitful thoughts of our minds against the Word of God".[362] A lie only has power when we assume it to be true.

Once Adam and Eve disobeyed God's command, the result was that they began to see things differently than they had before.[363] They realized they were naked which tells us that shame found a place within their hearts and minds for the first time. They tried dealing with the shame themselves – sewing fig leaves together and covering themselves with these temporary garments. They also attempted to hide from God[364] and when confronted, they placed the blame somewhere else.[365]

When we fall for the deception of the Enemy, our lives follow a similar pattern. We begin to doubt that God is acting in our best interests and we begin to believe the lie of Satan. Adam and Eve were not the only ones to follow this pattern; people throughout the ages have also fallen for it. Many examples are given throughout Scripture of Christians who have fallen for the deception of the Enemy - the Jewish people, the Israelites, the Pharisees, members of the churches Paul established, as well as scores of others. In the book of

---

[362] Robert McGee, *The Search for Significance* (Nashville, Word Publishing, 1998).

[363] Gen. 3:7

[364] Gen. 3:10

[365] Gen. 3:11-13

Romans, Paul even report that a number of the Gentile Christians had "exchanged the truth of God for a lie, and worshiped and served created things rather than the Creator.[366]" Let us take a look at what this means.

The word "exchange" in this passage comes from the Greek word *metallasso*, meaning to exchange one thing for another (or to change one thing with another). Previous to them believing the lie, we were told that their *thinking* had become futile and their foolish *hearts* were darkened.[367] The process that led to the acceptance of the lie (a "truth exchange") was that their thinking became futile, *mataioo*, meaning distorted, vain, empty, or useless and their foolish hearts were darkened *(skotizo)* and deprived of God's light. Do you see the disconnection that can take place between our logical, God-given thinking (based on His truth) and our heart (emotions and will) when there is distortion and a deficiency of God's light? We fail to respond in a god-given, healthy manner, as evidenced by the actions of the Gentiles. They lost their capacity to see and think clearly and reverted to sinful, addictive behavior.[368]

Remember, one of Satan's main schemes is distortion and once the thinking becomes distorted and the heart understanding is cut off from God's truth, we become prime candidates for idolatry (worship of idols). And then we are more easily drawn into worshipping and serving other things, allowing them to become our god. When our emotions aren't connected with our thinking (the truth of God), we are not likely to make godly choices.

How can we tell when we are being tempted to believe a lie instead of God's truth? Here are some possible clues that we might look for:

---

[366] Rom. 1:25

[367] Rom. 1:21

[368] Rom. 1:29-31

- We experience sudden anger or anxiety
- We have a hard time trusting God
- We struggle with some kind of fear in our life (fear of rejection/abandonment, fear of being alone, fear of death/dying, fear of commitment, fear of secrets being exposed, fear of scarcity, fear of failure, etc.)
- We feel shame, worthlessness, insecurity, defilement, hopelessness or depression
- We are upset when our perceived needs are not being met
- We give more priority to something other than God (mind, heart, and time)
- Walls of protection go up between us and God, and us and others
- We find substitutes for the love, acceptance, worth, and approval we need
- We try to cover up our shame and guilt
- We reap the consequences of worshiping and serving other things
- We turn to other things first, instead of God, when upset or frustrated
- We reach out to things, people, or processes in order to cover up our shame, trying to get them to sooth us and make us feel better
- We hide from God, when he reaches out to us, afraid he won't accept us because of what we have done

Have you noticed any of these clues in your life lately?

Chapter 20

The Healing Process

Did you know that for every lie that holds you captive, there is a truth that can set you free? We are reminded in John 8:32 that "You will know the truth and the truth will set you free". And that truth is based on what God says in His Word!

Replacing Lies with the Truth

Nancy DeMoss[369] offers five steps to use in exchanging Satan's lies for God's truth. In this way we can reverse the process that Satan has helped orchestrate in order to trap us.

1. IDENTIFY THE LIE. First, you must realize you are caught up in a lie and come into agreement with God that it is not his truth. Then you must identify the lie that you have believed *(I have believed the lie of Satan that [name lie])*

2. ACCEPT RESPONSIBILITY. Repent for worshipping and serving creative things other than God (because you have believed this lie). How has this lie(s) been evident in the way you have been living *(e.g. attitudes, actions, habits, addictions you turn to, emotional turmoil)*

3. EXCHANGE THE LIE FOR THE TRUTH. This is where you exchange the lie for the truth, affirming the truth. Speak the lie you've

---

[369] Nancy Leigh DeMoss, *Lies Women Believe and the Truth that Sets Them Free* (Chicago: Moody Publishers, 2001).

believed and then state the truth of God, based on scripture. *(I exchange Satan's lie for God's truth....)*

4. ACT ON THE TRUTH. What specific step(s) of action do you need to take to align your life with the Truth of God? *(Repentance, surrender, forgiving others, accountability, healing of hurts and wounds, etc.)*

5. ASK GOD TO HELP YOU WALK IN THE TRUTH. After you pray for his help, ask him to protect the truth you have affirmed. Read this truth over and over again for the next thirty days, especially when you feel the lie surfacing. I have also found it helpful to place this truth and the scripture that supports it on a small card that can be easily accessible for use.

Once you begin identifying the lies that you are being caught up in, you will realize that they are often the same ones. As you repeat this five-step process over and over you will begin to identify the lies sooner so that you can combat the enemy's schemes. This will give you a chance to apply God's Word immediately to the situation before the deception can set in and be acted out.

Taking time to memorize specific verses of God's Truth in his word can be God's armor (sword of the Spirit) against the enemy's lies.[370] Jesus himself was tempted with Satan's lies and he always combated those lies with the truth found in scripture.[371]

Let's look at some basic lies of Satan and God's truth that can set us free:

---

[370] Eph. 6:17

[371] Luke 4:1-13

166

Satan's Lies	God's Truth
Performance Trap. *I must meet certain standards to be worthwhile or to feel good about myself.*	Unconditional Love. *God loves me unconditionally for "who I am" not for what "I do".* [Rom. 5:8, Psa. 139:13-18, Matt. 10:29-31]
People Pleasing. *I must be accepted/approved by others to be worthwhile; what others think of me is what matters.*	Pleasing to God. *What God thinks about me is more important and is what makes me worthwhile.* [Gal. 1:10, I Thess. 2:4, Matt. 6:1, Jer. 17:5, 7, Isa. 43:1, 4, Rom. 8:31, Rom. 14:17-18, Isa. 49:15-16]
Fear of Failure. *Those who fail are unworthy of love; I must be perfect to be loveable.*	Perfect in Christ. *I am worth loving because of what Christ did, not for my failures.* [Rom. 8:1; I Jn. 3:1a; Isa. 64:6; II Cor. 12:9; Isa. 43:18-1, 9; Col 1:22]
I cannot Change. *I am flawed and defective; it's hopeless. I am covered with shame.*	Confident in Christ. *I am covered with Christ, not shame. His Power can help me change.* [Col. 2:10, Col. 3:9-10, Psa. 51:1-3, 17; Rom. 8:1-2, II Cor. 5:17, 21, Isa. 54:10, Psa. 42:5; Phil. 4:13, Isa. 45:24-25]
I am what I Have. *Possessions and appearance are what matters.*	I am Complete in Christ. *I am defined by who I am in Christ, not in what I have.* [I Sam. 16:7, Isa. 58:11, Psa. 39:14, Col 2:10 (KJV), Deut. 26:18]

What Adam and Eve got when they chose a way of being that was separate from God was the life of the false self. Any time we reject God or try to cope by ourselves, we end up with lies and frustration. But God wants to make provision for us just as he did for Adam and Eve. He made garments of skin for them from animals, more permanent than the fig leaves they had sown together. These skins, acquired through the death of an animal, became the first bloodshed to cover the sins of man. Eventually Jesus became a permanent sacrifice for all time, for all people,[372] allowing his blood to cover our sin and shame. Our part is to receive the covering that Christ has provided for us so that we can return to our true self-created in his image.

Inner Healing Prayer

As we consider soul wounds we are reminded of the words of David, "He leads me beside quiet waters, He *restores my soul.*"[373]

In order to heal the wounds or hurts from the past we must come to God in prayer because he is the real Healer. Here is a type of process that can be useful. *Remember that past hurts can be painful and it might be important to have someone present with you during a process such as this.*

- Close your eyes and relax in God's presence.
- Ask the Holy Spirit to identify the hurt or wound that took place in the past. Then in your memory, go back to the time and place of the hurt.
- In prayer, tell Jesus about the situation that was hurtful and what feelings you experienced. (You may need to grieve this loss or hurt before the Lord as well.)
- Then ask Christ to heal the wound, filling the wound with His presence and strength.
- Allow yourself to sit quietly in God's presence: What are you sensing? What are you seeing? What are you

---

[372] Rom. 6:10, Heb. 7:27, I Pet. 3:18

[373] Ps. 23:2-3 [italics added].

168

hearing from God? (you may sense a feeling, see a picture, or hear God saying something to you)

- What did you believe as a result of this hurt that has created emotional turmoil in you? (false belief or lie) How did you react as a result of this hurt? (dysfunctional behavior)
- Exchange this lie for God's truth (see process for this in the beginning of Chapter 20.
- Finally, thank God and celebrate what he has done! Ask God to seal (and protect) what he has done in you so the enemy cannot deceive you anymore with his lies. (For more information on this process of healing, see additional resource section at the end of this section.)

Other Steps for Healing

Other steps in this healing process involve forgiveness to those who have hurt you, acknowledgement and confession of generational sins, and the breaking of any soul wounds that have hurt you. According to Exodus 20:5, generational sins are passed down to the third and fourth generation. But we are also reminded that we were redeemed from our futile way of life inherited from our forefather with the blood of Christ.[374]

Chester and Betsy Kylstra give us this definition of generational sins.

Sins of the fathers represent the accumulation of all sins committed by our ancestors. It is the heart tendency (iniquity) that we inherit from our forefathers to rebel against God's laws and commandments. It is the propensity to sin, particularly in ways that represent perversion and twisted character.[375]

---

[374] I Pet. 1:18-19 [NAB].

169

Some of the frequently occurring sins of the fathers found within families include things such as: abandonment, abuse (emotional, physical, or sexual), addictions, anger, control, manipulation, emotional dependency, fear, idolatry, money issues, physical infirmities, pride, rebellion, rejection, insecurity, sexual sin, unbelief, and inferiority[376]. The Scriptures give direction concerning the freedom we can find from generational sin.[377] Kylstras' offer us a process for dealing these generational sins. 1) Identify and confess the sins of your fathers, 2) Forgive your ancestors for all the sins they committed that have affected your life, 3) Ask and receive God's forgiveness for your part in entering into and yielding to the sins of your fathers, 4) Refuse any more involvement in these sins, and 5) Apply the power of the cross and the blood of Christ to cover you and protect what you have done in this regard.

Most ungodly beliefs (or lies) are formed in hurtful situations. They can result from hurtful family patterns or things done or said to us. Healing must take place before our belief can be rebuilt on God's truth. If our mind is being renewed[378] saying "I'm healed or being transformed" but our heart says, "I'm hurting", which one do you think will win out? It is usually the heart. Satan loves to stir up the same hurts by picking off the scabs or arranging events to cause more hurt within us. So, allow God to heal the hurt so his truth can fully settle into our hearts.

---

[375]Chester and Betsy Kylstra, *Biblical healing and deliverance* (Grand Rapids, MI: Chosen Books, 2005).

[376] Ibid.

[377] Lev. 26:40-42, Dan. 9:4-19

[378] Rom. 12:2

Chapter 21

The Components of Change

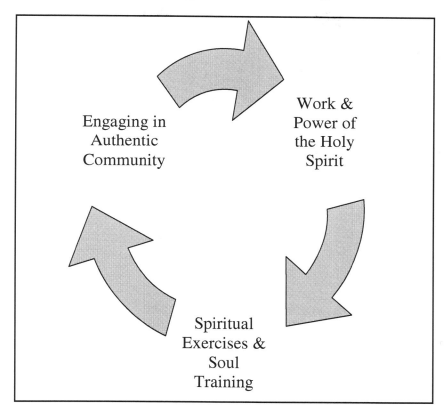

Any change we make will only last a short while if it is done by our own effort. For real, lasting change only takes place through the power of the Holy Spirit. That is why this diagram begins with the "work and power of the Holy Spirit". There is no other substitute that will work! We must also spend time with God, building a meaningful relationship with him. We must also get involved in supportive relationships that will help support our walk with Christ.

Believe me; I have walked this journey of healing. During a difficult time in my life I tried everything I could think of in order to change: bargaining with God, pleading with others, creative problem solving, naming and claiming what I wanted, self-help book techniques, obsessively reading the bible, blaming others, isolating myself, etc. But none of this really worked. I remember standing in my bedroom one day during this difficult time and saying to myself, "Gwen you are either going to lose your mind or surrender this to God." My biggest concern was that if I allowed God to be in charge, he would not change my situation the way I wanted him to. I have found that we will generally not change until it is more uncomfortable to stay the same than to change. I call this my time of desperation! Desperation took me to a place where I was ready to do it God's way.

Jesus often had people asking him for advice. For instance, the disciples wanted to know who was the greatest. Jesus surprised them when he called a little child over, stood him in the middle of the room and said to them, "Unless you change and become like little children, you will never enter the kingdom of heaven."[379] A paraphrased translation, the Message, says it this way, "I'm telling you, once and for all, that unless you return to square one and start over like children, you're not even going to get a look at the kingdom, let alone get in. Whoever becomes simple and elemental again, like this child, will rank high in God's kingdom." What was Jesus really saying to the disciples? He was reminding them that children are open, transparent, honest, loving, simple-minded, and not sufficient in themselves. He was calling them to humbleness and humility. Jesus had been modeling, and would continue to model, how to be humble: forget yourself, love others, take on the form of a servant, live a self-less obedient life, die to yourself and serve others.[380]

---

[379] Matt. 18:3

[380] Phil. 2:2-8

Another time Jesus was asked by a rich young ruler what he needed to do in order to inherit eternal life. Jesus looked at him with love and said the last thing the man wanted to hear, "Go sell whatever you own and give it to the poor. All your wealth will then be heavenly wealth.[381] The man walked away with a heavy heart because he was holding on tight to a lot of things and not about to let them go.

The Components

Our surrender to God gives permission for the Holy Spirit to release his power and begin his work in our lives. Then God can use spiritual exercises and disciplines to help bring us into a stronger relationship with him *(check out the spiritual exercises in Part two and in Appendix B for help in this area),* and soul work that can help us heal the lies and wounds that have held us captive. This process sets in motion our dependence on him and his truth. As we begin listening to him, we will hear his voice and it will let us know - one day at a time - how to walk this healing journey.

Then as we grow more and more in love with Christ, we will begin to long for authentic community. It is dangerous to go it alone! "If one falls down, his friend can help him up...Though one may be overpowered, two can defend themselves. A cord of three strands is not easily broken.[382]" Community must also include the Triune God (Father, Son, and Holy Spirit) who also exists in community. With these two types of community we can become empowered and transformed people who will glorify God and then be able to encourage and challenge others in love (Heb. 10:24) and reach out to those in need (Gal. 6:2, I Pet. 4:8, Matt. 22:37).

---

[381] Mark 10:21 [MSG].

[382] Eccl. 4:10-12

173

GOING DEEPER ⇓

Reflection Questions *(for Individuals or a Group)*

CONNECTING WITH GOD
Think of a place that feels safe to you and visit there in your mind. During the beginning moments of silence, purposefully invite Jesus to be in that place with you.

THINKING OUTLOUD
Open your heart to the healing God has for you this week.

1. Read the baby crab story (in this section) out loud. Many times we adopt a pretend self (a mask or false self) in order to hide. Or we will act and respond in ways that we think others want us to, losing our true self in the process.
   - As in the story of the baby crab, there is a huge price to be paid if we settle for the protection of the false self. Describe that price.
   - How does a mask or false self keep us from experiencing authentic community?
   - As you look at the list of traits of the True Self and False Self, what do you see as the main differences?
   - What do you think is the process for taking off the mask and living as the person God made you to be?
2. Review the list of lies in Chapter 19 and the clues that may indicate that you believe a lie.
   - What is one of the lies that you presently believe. (Use the process in this section to identify God's truth for this lie.) Why is it important to deal with lies in your life (Jn. 8:44)
3. Discuss the "Components of Change" in Chapter 21.
   - Why are all three of these components important ingredients in change?
   - Which of the three components are the most difficult to include in your life? Which component would you like to grow in the most right now?

- Jesus summarized all the commandments into just two (Matt. 22:37-40). How do the components of change relate and agree with the commandments (or priorities) of Jesus?

BEING FORMED BY THE WORD

- Using Zephaniah 3:17 lead the group in a formational time using "Experiencing the Heart of God" (Appendix B).

PRAYING FOR GOD'S HEART

Healing Prayer *(You may want to do the next three bullet points in 2's and allow this experience to be the closing prayer so that each group of 2's can end when they are through.)*
- Share something that someone said (or did) to you as a child that was hurtful and has stuck with you.
- Identify the lie that you believed because of this hurt and the way it has trapped you or limited you in some way (like the baby crab)?
- Share with each other the hurt and the lie you believed. Then pray with each other for God's healing of the hurt. (If you are comfortable, use the process of inner healing prayer that was described in this section.)
- Purpose to pray for each other this week and the struggle you are having in becoming Holy and Whole in Spirit.

TAKING TIME TO BE FORMED

First Day:

Anger is a secondary emotion that we experience in response to a primary emotion. Three of the primary emotions that may be the actual source of our anger are *hurt, frustration, or fear.* These emotions are felt when our goals, values, and expectations are not met or when our *personal worth* is threatened. So, anger is really a "warning sign" that one of these primary emotions have surfaced in the form of our anger. Try these ideas:

- The next time you feel angry, take time to reflect on the source of that anger. Try to identify the primary emotion beneath your anger. Is it hurt, frustration or fear? Is your personal worth being threatened? Journal about this situation.
- There are three ways people deal with their anger:
  1. repress it (consciously unaware of it)
  2. suppress it (aware of it, but choose to hold it inside)
  3. express it in a healthy way (How do you express it?)

Second Day:

Take a look at one or two of the boundary issues indicated by the Boundaries Self-test. Use some of these ways for processing what this might say to you:

a) Discuss this issue with a friend or counselor. Do they see this as an issue in your life? What might you do about it?

b) Journal about this issue. After journaling, spend some time in meditation and prayer. Allow God to speak to you during the time of meditation.

c) Using a concordance, look for scriptures that might speak to this boundary issue in your life. Meditate on the scripture/s and listen to what God is saying to you and how he wants you to act in response.

Third Day:

Check out the list of traits of the false self and the true self found in this chapter. Identify several traits of the false self that you find in your life? What might you do to become more of your true self?

Fourth Day:

Write a journal entry reflecting on the way in which you have embraced "lies" in your life through circumstances or people's words. Describe some ways your hurts and lies have hindered your relationship with God?

Fifth Day:

Make a list of some of the generational patterns that are found in your family line (see the list given in this section on emotional wholeness). Reflect on the list you made. How are these patterns evident in your life? How have they affected you and your relationships with others? How have they affected your walk with God?

Bibliography

Benner, David. *The Gift of Being Yourself*. Downers Grove, IL: InterVarsity Press. 2004.

DeMoss, Nancy Leigh. *Lies Women Believe and the Truth that Sets them Free*. Chicago: Moody Publishers, 2001.

Eldredge, John. *Waking the Dead: The Glory of a Heart Fully Alive*. Nashville: Nelson Books, 2003.

Gerlach, Peter K, "Who Runs Your Life?" Break the Cycle. http://sfhelp.org/01/f+t_selves.htm (accessed August 9, 2008).

Holtz, Talbert. *Street Wisdom: Connecting with God in Everyday Life*. Mystic, CT: Twenty-Third Publications, 2003.

Kylstra, Chester and Betsy. *Biblical Healing and Deliverance*. Grand Rapids, MI: Chosen Books, 2005.

McGee, Robert. *The Search for Significance*. Nashville: Word Publishing. 1998.

Merton, Thomas. *New Seeds of Contemplation*. New York: New Directions. 1961.

Norman, Wright. 2003. *The New Guide to Crisis & Trauma Counseling*. Ventura, CA: Regal Books.

Steinke, Peter. *How Your Church Family Works*. Washington, DC: Alban Institute, 1993.

Young, William. *The Shack*. LosAngeles: Windblown Media, 2007.

Additional Resources

Allender, Dan B. *The Healing Path: How the Hurts in your Past can lead you to a more Abundant Life*. Colorado Springs, CO: WaterBrook Press, 1999.

Barton, Ruth Haley. *The Truths that Free Us*. Colorado Springs: WaterBrook Press, 2002.

Cloud, Henry and John Townsend. *Boundaries*. Grand Rapids, MI: Zondervan, 2002.

Faulkner, Brooks and Guy Greenfield. *The Wounded Minister*. Grand Rapids, MI: Baker, 2001.

Hart, Archibald. *Adrenaline and Stress*. Dallas: Word, 1995.

Nouwen, Henri J. M. *The Inner Voice of Love: A Journey through Anguish to Freedom,* New York: Random House, Inc., 1996.

Scazzero, Peter. *Emotionally healthy spirituality*. Nashville: Thomas Nelson, Inc., 2006.

Scazzero, Peter. *The Emotionally Healthy Church*. Grand Rapids, MI: Zondervan, 2004.

Swenson, Richard. *The Overload Syndrome: Learning to Live Within Your Limits*. Colorado Springs: NavPress, 1999.

Thurman, Chris. *The Lies We Believe*. Nashville: Thomas Nelson, Inc., 1989.

Thom Gardner. *Healing the Wounded Heart: Removing Obstacles to Intimacy with God*. Shippensburg, PA: Destiny Image Publishers, 2005.

Wardle, Terry. *Healing Care, Healing Prayer: Helping the Broken Find Wholeness in Christ.* Abilene, TX: Leafwood Publishers, 2001.

Wilson, Michael Todd and Brad Hoffmann. *Preventing Ministry Failure: A ShepherdCare Guide for Pastors, Ministers, and Other Caregivers.* Downers Grove, IL: InterVarsity Press, 2007.

Wilson, Sandra D. *Into Abba's Arms: Finding the Acceptance You've always Wanted.* Wheaton, IL: Tyndale House Publishers, 1998.

Part V

HOLY AND WHOLE: In Sexuality

Therefore a man leaves his father and mother and embraces his wife. They become one flesh. The two of them, the man and his Wife, were naked, but they felt no shame.
-Genesis 2:24-25 [MSG]

God designed marital sex to be an encounter with the divine...Sex was to be the way that a husband and wife were to touch each other's soul.
-Tim Gardner[383]

Being holy and whole is especially critical in the area of sexuality for Christians in today's culture. The beliefs of the culture about sexuality have slowly crept into the church until what Christians believe about sexuality has very little resemblance to what the Scriptures say.

Paul reminds us in his letter to the Thessalonians, "God's will is for you to be holy, so stay away from all sexual sin. Then each of you will control his own body and live in holiness and honor – not in lustful passion like the pagans who do not know God and his ways."[384]

---

[383] Tim Alan Gardner, Sacred Sex: A Spiritual Celebration of Oneness in Marriage (Colorado Springs: Waterbrook Press, 2002), 5.

[384] I Thess. 4:3-5 [NLT].

Chapter 22

Authentic Sexuality

As we look for guidance in the Scriptures, we discover several principles concerning sexuality. First, according to Genesis 2:25, sexuality was created before the fall and took place between the "man and his wife." Sexuality in Genesis 2 was shared by a man and a woman, but not only male and female, but a man and his *wife*. A committed heterosexual relationship, sealed and witnessed by the vows of marriage, provides the safest place for sexual intimacy and constitutes God's original design. God's plan was not to keep us from this intimacy, but to protect the beautiful gift he gave us until the day we were united as husband and wife.

In Gen. 2:18 God says, "It is not good for man to be alone. I will make a helper suitable for him." God desired for Adam to have a mate who was designed for him, a companion that was "just right for him."[385] Within a few verses, we find out who that suitable helper is – a woman.[386]

Secondly, it is clear that God designated sex to be sacred and holy. The word holy describes something that has been designed by God as holy and has been set apart by God and for God. It also means "to evoke adoration, worship, and even fear and trembling."[387] God elected at creation to have sex play the holy role of creating oneness between a wife and her husband. But the oneness, the unity, was and is created by God Himself, not by a mere physical act.[388]

---

[385] Gen. 2:18 [NLT].

[386] Gen. 2:22

[387] Gardner, 9.

[388] Ibid., 39.

Here's another reason why sex is holy. It can usher us into a genuine experience of worship. Just as the appearance of the burning bush filled Moses with awe, the true experience of oneness…can bring us to a place of heartfelt praise and adoration of Him. It can leave us trembling at the wonder and beauty and love of almighty God, who gave us this incredible gift.[389]

Saying that sex is holy can seem ridiculous when we realize all the ways that sex does not appear *holy* in our culture today. "Our sex-saturated culture worships bodies, focuses on individual pleasures, and glorifies sex outside of marriage"[390] They mainly see satisfaction and orgasm as the goal and expect that a couple will have sex soon after a couple begins dating. But the sacredness of sex is not "based on how we treat it or mistreat it. Its sacredness is based on its essence, which comes from God. Sex is holy because God created it to be holy"[391] He Himself is present whenever a wife and husband partake of His gift of sex. This is especially noticeable to couples who are committed to Christ and have committed their relationship to him.

Third, the primary goal of sex is not procreation or pleasure, but to create and celebrate a sacred intimacy – a "oneness" or a uniting of two into one flesh. The uniting of the two involves a man leaving his father and mother and being *united* with his wife[392] This uniting enables the couple to weave their lives together through a type of communion, establishing closeness in the relationship.

Becoming one flesh indicates intimacy in the fullest sense, but especially in regard to sexuality because this

---

[389] Ibid., 10.

[390] Ibid., 12.

[391] Ibid., 8.

[392] Gen. 2:24 [italics added].

ordinance is followed by the words, "the man and his wife were both naked, and they felt no shame."[393] They were perfectly comfortable with this gift of intimacy that God had given them - no shame, no hiding, no need to protect themselves. Isn't it interesting that Eve is first created physically from his rib and declared to be flesh "of" his flesh, and then, after the words of Genesis 2:24, they are described as becoming not just flesh of his flesh, but "one flesh" together?

There are several possible implications of "one flesh". Becoming one flesh could indicate a spiritual connection. Adam first had a spiritual connection with God and so did Eve and then he and Eve together have a relationship with God. The strongest relationship is formed when husband, wife, and God are linked together. "A triple-braided cord is not easily broken.[394]" If you image the marriage relationship as a triangle with husband and wife on the base and God at the apex, then as each person focuses on and grows toward God, they also grow closer to each other.

Most couples I meet struggle more with being spiritually intimate with one another than being sexually intimate. Studying God's word together, praying to God, admitting one's shortcomings & sins, and admitting one's need for God can make us feel very vulnerable. But a spiritual connection is a strength that can and will strengthen every other part of the relationship, especially sexual intimacy.

Another possibility is that one flesh speaks of the emotional connection of two people. In the process of growing the relationship, they look into each other's eyes and into each other's hearts and into each other's souls. They become "soul mates" and have a close, intimate relationship. They feel comfortable sharing their feelings and emotions with each

---

[393] Gen. 2:25

[394] Eccl. 4:12 [NLT].

187

other. Hence, they are "naked and unashamed" emotionally as well as physically.

Finally, it may refer to the sexual union, which most theologians believe "one flesh" indicates. Paul gives us an idea of this meaning when he says these words, "Do you not know that he who *unites* himself with a prostitute is one (flesh) with her in body?[395]

When sex takes place between a man and a prostitute, a person he barely knows, it creates a type of bodily oneness. No wonder sex outside of marriage (adultery) creates a disturbance to the connection of a relationship! A conflicting type of bodily oneness has been introduced into the relationship that disrupts the original marital oneness.

Is it any wonder that the breaking of the marriage covenant takes place through *sexual unfaithfulness* with someone else besides the partner, often ending up in a divorce or the death of the marriage? When you tear apart something that is bonded, it is not a clean tear – it is a rip.

Unfaithfulness, as well as divorce, leaves us with a painful tear that is not easy to heal. God is protecting us when he tells us to keep sex "in the fireplace" (or the marriage relationship) where it belongs and is safe. Fire outside the fireplace can destroy and so can sex outside of the marriage relationship. Satan loves it when he can destroy a marriage and tear apart the bond that God is creating between a husband and wife.

In Dutch, the word for sex is the word "naaien" which literally means "sewing". This gives us a picture of two pieces of material that are put on top of each other and sewn together in order to keep the two fabrics connected securely together, long after the sewer is gone. So in the case of marriage, we get the picture of two people sewn together by God through sexual intimacy, a process that unites them.

---

[395] I Cor. 6:16 [italics added].

188

When Paul refers to this creation ordinance from Genesis, he adds these words, "This is a profound mystery..."[396] He goes on to give us a clearer understanding of this mystery by comparing the marriage relationship with the relationship between Christ and his church.[397]

In this metaphor, we are reminded of the mystery of this sacred gift between Christ and the church, as well as a husband and his wife, in the areas of unconditional love,[398] loving care,[399] respect and support,[400] and faithfulness,[401] reminding us that this gift can be tainted by conditional love, uncaring actions, selfishness, and unfaithfulness.

Our sexuality was designed to be the greatest parable of the ultimate love story – God's great love for us. Sexual intercourse between husband and wife is to reflect God's love for us – pure, priceless, and protected from all who seek to destroy it. [402]

Intimacy, along with commitment and faithful love, was the design of a Creator who wanted to protect the relationship shared between a husband and wife. What a thoughtful design God had when he created marriage to be initiated by a covenant, nourished by spiritual, emotional, and physical

---

[396] Eph. 5:32

[397] Eph. 5:32

[398] Eph. 5:25-28

[399] Eph. 5:29-30

[400] Eph. 5:23, 33

[401] Eph. 5:3

[402] Doub Rosenau and Michael Todd Wilson, *Soul Virgins: Redefining Single Sexuality* (Grand Rapids: BakerBooks, 2006), 69.

intimacy, and supported by grace, openness, vulnerability, and faithfulness! Emotional intimacy creates closeness and trust; spiritual intimacy creates connection between the husband, the wife, and God; while physical intimacy acts as the glue that binds all of it together.

Fourth, marriage is to be viewed as a covenant. A covenant, according to Scripture, contained two parts: a verbal declaration and a spoken vow. For Noah God's vow was to never flood the earth again,[403] and the oath sign was a rainbow that sealed the deal.[404] In marriage, the verbal declaration is the spoken vows made at the time of the wedding ceremony. The oath sign today is the ring and the kiss, the actions that signify the sealing of the deal. However, according to Jewish tradition the wedding canopy represented an oath sign that was seen as an actual part of the wedding.[405] After their vows, the wedded couple was escorted into a private room so that they could consummate the marriage with the act of sexual intercourse.

As far as God is concerned, sexual intimacy is still the oath sign. As a husband and a wife are described as two individuals leaving their homes and becoming one – and as becoming one always refers to sexual intimacy – then the sign of the covenant of marriage is, in fact, the consummation.[406] So, in this sense, sexual intimacy between a husband and wife

---

[403] Gen. 9:11

[404] Gen. 9:13

[405] B. Greenberg, "Marriage in the Jewish Tradition," *Journal of Ecumenical Studies* 22, no. 1 (1985).

[406] Tim A. Gardner, "Developing a Practical Theology of Sex," *Marriage and Family* 5 (2002):364.

is not only what establishes the covenant, but is also a sign of the ongoing renewal of the covenant[407]

How can we apply this to our marriage? One way is to remember that every time a married person enters into sexual intimacy they are repeating the oath sign, just as God does when he sends a rainbow after a storm. They are in essence saying, "I do". "I am committed to you and to this marriage." "I am restating my commitment to you that I will love you forever." "I am renewing the covenant I made to you at the wedding ceremony." So, each act of sexual intimacy not only signifies the original oath sign, but is the ongoing renewal of the marriage covenant.

In addition, Tim Gardner mentions the following applications:

- When you are pushing your spouse for sex, ask yourself these questions, "Will this pressure I am putting on my spouse promote oneness or cause division? Am I being selfish or selfless?
- Seeing sex as a renewal of the covenant and as an act of serving moves sex from a duty or a boring act to an act of love and a chance to partake in the "profound mystery"[408] and to honor the love God has created and given.
- In the case of someone suffering from sexual abuse or sexual addiction, having a healthy theology of sexuality can help one see the difference between the abuse of God's gift and its proper meaning and use.
- Finally, in viewing the sexual act in this God-honoring way, we will begin seeing our mates, not as objects to satisfy us, but rather as God's perfect gift to us.

---

[407] J.F. Kippley, *Sex and the Marriage Covenant: A Basis for Morality.* Cincinnati, OH: The Couple to Couple League International, Inc., 1991.

[408] Eph. 5:32

Tim Gardner asserts that "more conflict arises within the sexual relationship due to faulty and selfish views of sexuality... (than with) biological impediments or miscues."[409] Selflessness gives without expectation, loves without conditions, forgives seventy times seven, offers sexual intimacy in order to show love, and guards the marital relationship by choosing to be accountable to others.

Paul gives additional meaning to sex and oneness with the following words:

> There is more to sex than mere skin on skin. Sex is as much spiritual mystery as physical fact...Since we want to become spiritually one with the Master, we must not pursue the kind of sex that avoids commitment and intimacy, leaving us more lonely than ever – the kind of sex that can never "become one." There is a sense in which sexual sins are different from all others. In sexual sin we violate the sacredness of our own bodies, these bodies that were made for God-given and God-modeled love, for "becoming one" with another.[410]

In the book, *Soul Virgins,* Rosenau and Wilson explain that sexuality has five different types of sexual expression (or spokes) that help create this oneness: spiritual, emotional, mental, social, and physical. These spokes, containing both erotic and non-erotic expressions, must all be considered if we are going to embrace wholeness in the area of marital intimacy.[411]

---

[409] Ibid., 359.

[410] I Cor. 6:16-18 [MSG].

[411] Doub Rosenau and Michael Todd Wilson, *Soul Virgins: Redefining Single Sexuality* (Grand Rapids: BakerBooks, 2006).

Instead of being independent of one another they see the spokes as complementary and interactive, which creates a balanced wheel.

Balance is crucial in developing well-rounded intimacy in relationships. When one spoke is larger (or smaller) than the rest, the wheel becomes out of round and will eventually cause extensive damage – not only to the wheel (sexual wholeness) but potentially to the vehicle itself (relationship)...This five-spoked intimacy produces a mature *sexual wholeness,* reflecting God's intimate best.[412]

A well-balanced wheel, embracing all five types of sexual expression, can also help safeguard the marriage relationship from the temptation to have sex with someone other than the marriage partner. This is essential, especially since there are many consequences that result from sexuality that occur outside of God's designed plan: calamity and backlash in one's own family,[413] physical and spiritual death,[414] godly punishment,[415] hardness of heart and divorce,[416] hurt, an inability to bond with another partner afterwards, and more vulnerability to future sexual indiscretion. God's way of sexuality is the best and the most fulfilling!

Controlling sexual lust has never been easy in any culture or at any time. We are all vulnerable to the temptation of

---

[412] Ibid., 227-228.

[413] II Sam. 12:9-12

[414] I Cor. 10:8

[415] I Thess. 4:4-6

[416] Matt. 19:4-9

sexual lust and sin[417] and we are tempted when by our own evil desire, we are dragged away and enticed.[418] But, "God is faithful; he will not let you be tempted beyond what you can bear. But when you are tempted, he will also provide a way out so that you can stand up under it."[419]

God calls us to take a proactive stand in the area of sexuality. Here are some things to consider:

1. Stay as far away as you can from any obvious sexual temptation[420]
2. Find healing from any sexual abuse in your past
3. Deal with sexual addiction issues in your life
4. Make your relationship with God a daily priority
5. Find accountability (with a person of the same sex, a small group, accountability software, etc.)
6. Guard your heart[421]
7. Deal with your view of God and self
8. Deal with faulty body image issues
9. Become aware of the differences between the culture's view of sexuality and God's unique plan
10. Surrender your body to the Holy Spirit

Finally, listen to Paul's words as he challenges us concerning our bodies, "the temple" of the Lord:

Didn't you realize that your body is a sacred place, the place of the Holy Spirit? Don't you see that you can't

---

[417] I Cor. 10:13b

[418] James 1:14

[419] I Cor. 10:13

[420] I Thess. 5:22 [KJV].

[421] Prov. 4:23

live however you please, squandering what God paid such a high price for? The physical part of you is not some piece of property belonging to the spiritual part of you. God owns the whole works. So let people see God in and through your body.[422]

---

[422] I Cor. 6:19-20 [MSG].

GOING DEEPER ⇓

Reflection Questions *(for Individuals or a Group)*

CONNECTING WITH GOD
Sit in silence for five minutes. Invite God to speak to your heart during this session.

THINKING OUTLOUD
Take time to not only answer these questions but to ask your own questions about the primary ideas of this section.

1. Why do you think the church (or Christian people) avoids or simply fails to talk and teach about God's plan for sexuality?
2. Discuss the following statements by Phillip Yancey[423]:
   - "Every man who knocks on the door of a brothel is (really) looking for God".
   - "Because marriage is a sacrament, every test of fidelity poses a *spiritual test* as well as a moral one".
3. Sexual intimacy between a husband & a wife was always meant to *be a reflection* of the intimacy between the groom (Jesus Christ) and His bride - the church. Read Eph. 5:23, 25-32; Isa. 62:5; Rev. 19:7-8; and Rev. 21:2.
   - How do these scriptures inform us about how God intends for our relationship to be with our mates?
   - If our relationship with our mate is a reflection of the intimacy between us and Christ, then how we treat our mates, how we show them love, and how we approach them sexually is a way of responding to this God we worship. How do you feel about this statement?
4. Oneness involves five different types of sexual expression: spiritual, emotional, mental, social, and physical, each feeding and affecting the other. Each one needs to be considered if we

---

[423]Yancey, Philip. *Designer Sex.* Downers Grove, IL: InterVarsity Press, 2005.

are to embrace wholeness in the area of marriage and sexuality.

- Discuss the concept of the five spokes that Rosenau and Wilson talk about. What can we do if we struggle being intimate in one area (for instance: emotional)?
- It has been said that spiritual intimacy can encourage (or lead into) sexual intimacy. Why might this be true?

BEING FORMED BY THE WORD

- Have each person do the spiritual formation exercise, *Praying the Scripture* (from Appendix B) with I Corinthians 13:4-7.
- If you are single, apply it to a relationship in your life. If you are married, think in reference to your spouse.

PRAYING FOR GOD'S HEART (Chose one of the options)

- As you close, have couples pray together with their spouses.
- Or use this prayer in closing: *(my adaptation of I Cor. 13:4-7)*

Lord, I am bankrupt without love.
I need your help in loving more for others than for myself;
In not wanting what I don't have;
In being jealous, boastful, proud, or rude.
May I think of others instead of demanding my own way;
Help me not to fly off the handle
or keep score of the wrongs of others.
Help me instead to rejoice whenever the truth wins out.
May I trust you always and never give up.
May I always look for the best.
And never look back, but keep going to the end!
Amen.

TAKING TIME TO BE FORMED

First Day:

Journal about these questions:
- How did you first learn about sexuality?
- Were you ever aware of the biblical understanding of sexuality (presented in this section)?
- What information in this section was most helpful for you?

Second Day:

Continue the journaling you began on the First Day.
- Have you ever been hurt or violated in the area of sexuality? If so, when and how did it happen? Have you ever shared this with someone else?
- What is your greatest struggle in the area of sexuality? Have you ever shared this with another person? (Consider sharing either of the above two things with a trusted friend, clergy, or counselor this week.)
- Ask God's help in any area in which you struggle about sexuality.

Third Day:

Take time to look at the five areas of your life: spiritual, emotional, mental, social, and physical.
- Which of these areas are the hardest for you in relating to your spouse (or with your friends or family)?
- Write down one particular area in which you would like to grow.
- Pray for God's guidance in this area.
- Look back at some of the resources in the particular sections of this book (in that area) to find ways to address the thing that is hardest for you.

Fourth Day:

Remember that we will struggle in relationships with other people if God is not the priority of our lives.
- Begin by surrendering your struggle with relationships to God and listen for what he wants to say to you.
- Go back to Part II, Holy and Whole in Spirit, in finding some help in ways to spend time with God.
- Are you willing to commit to spend more time with God? (If not, what is taking away your appetite for being with God?)

Fifth Day:

At the end of this section on sexuality, there were some suggestions for taking a proactive stand in the area of sexuality. Reread through those suggestions.
- Pick one or two that you would like to focus on this week.
- Reread the following scripture from I Corinthians 6:19-20 [MSG] that was written in this section and pray back to God what stands out to you.

Didn't you realize that your body is a
sacred place, the place of the Holy Spirit?
Don't you see that you can't live however you please,
squandering what God paid such a high price for?
The physical part of you is not some piece of property
belonging to the spiritual part of you.
God owns the whole works.
So let people see God in and through your body.

Bibliography

Gardner, Tim A. "Developing a Practical Theology of Sex." *Marriage & Family: A Christian Journal* 5 (2002): 359-366.

Greenberg, B. "Marriage in the Jewish Tradition." *Journal of Ecumenical Studies* 22, no.1 (1985): 3-20.

Kippley, J.F. *Sex and the Marriage Covenant: A Basis for Morality.* Cincinnati, OH: The Couple to Couple League International, Inc., 1991.

Rosenau, Doug and Michael Todd Wilson. *Soul Virgins: Redefining Single Sexuality.* Grand Rapids: BakerBooks, 2006.

Additional Resources

Penner, Clifford, and Joyce Penner. *Getting your Sex Life off to a Great Start.* Nashville: Thomas Nelson, 199

Epilogue

Growth in wholeness is a process and will not take place without a growing relationship with Christ, trials to challenge you, friends to support you, and a faith to sustain you. And God will not work in you, to change you, without your permission. Growing toward spiritual, physical, and emotional wholeness will come at a cost to you. You will need to deny yourself and take up your cross,[424] surrender yourself to God, give him your possessions, your time, your will, your desires, your hopes, and your dreams.

Many changes have taken place in my life in recent years – a change of vocational focus from pastoral ministry to seminary professor, a marital separation that lasted for three and a half years concluding in a divorce, the death of several dear friends and relatives, several moves, new friends, and eventually a new husband! At first my life did not feel normal with all these changes, but as time went on I began to embrace God's future and hope for me.[425] I could then trust that every detail in my life of love for God would be worked into something good.[426]

One day as I was thinking about what had taken place in my life, I found this scripture from Isaiah that described it so well:

Because you scorn this Message, preferring to live by injustice and *shape your lives on lies*, this perverse way of life will be a towering, badly built wall that *slowly, slowly tilts and shifts*, and then one day, without warning, *collapses* – smashed to bits like a piece of pottery, smashed beyond recognition or repair, useless, a pile of debris to be swept up and thrown in the trash. God the

---

[424] Mark 8:34

[425] Jer. 29:11

[426] Rom. 8:28

Master, The Holy of Israel, has this solemn counsel: "Your salvation requires you to turn back to me and *stop your silly efforts to save yourselves.* Your strength will come from *settling down in complete dependence on me.*[427]

Another version describes the origin of our strength in this way, "in quietness and trust is your strength."[428] Through spending time with God, I have acquired a quietness of heart and a peacefulness that defies the crazy happenings of this life. I have learned to turn back toward God in trust every time life tests me. God has challenged me with these words, "Forget the former things; do not dwell on the past. See I am doing a new thing! Now it springs up; do you not perceive it? I am making a way in the desert and streams in the wasteland.[429]

I have learned that God is always faithful and that we can turn toward him whenever life does not make sense. I love the third verse of the hymn, *Great is thy Faithfulness*, based on Lamentations 3:22 and 23. It speaks of his presence and his strength that offers us a bright hope for tomorrow!

Pardon for sin and a peace that endureth,
Thine own dear presence to cheer and to guide,
Strength for today and bright hope for tomorrow.
Blessings all mine, with ten thousand beside!

Great is thy faithfulness, Great is thy faithfulness,
Morning by morning new mercies I see;
All I have needed thy hand hath provided.
Great is thy faithfulness, Lord, unto me!

---

[427] Isa. 30:12-15 [MSG, italics added].

[428] Isa. 30:15 [NIV].

[429] Isa. 43:18-19

One of the ways that God's faithfulness came to me was in this promise which can be yours, too. "I know the plans I have for you, plans to prosper you and not to harm you, plans to give you hope and a future."[430]

But this is what he asks of you. "Then you will call upon me and come and pray to me, and I will listen to you. You will seek me and find me when you seek me with *all your heart*."[431] As you do this he promises, "I will be found by you and bring you back from captivity."[432] We have all been captives, but the promise is that he will rescue us and walk with us on this journey toward being mature and complete.[433]

I would love to hear about your journey of growth. You can contact me at gebner@winebrenner.edu. or via my website www.PersonalGrowthForMe.com, a website that can also assist you on your own journey of personal growth.

God bless you as you journey toward being "holy and whole". It is a journey that begins one day at a time, but is the ride of a lifetime!

---

[430] Jer. 29:11

[431] Jer. 29;12-13 [italics added].

[432] Jer. 29:14

[433] Jas. 1:4

Appendix A - View of God
Assessment Tools

View of God Assessment

Place a checkmark by the statements that apply to you *right now*
Then place a checkmark by the ones that applied to you *as a Child*

	My Feelings about God...	Right now...	As a child...
*	I am afraid of God		
*	God is rigid and strict		
#	God isn't reliable and doesn't come through for me		
+	God is approachable		
+	God is a loving father		
#	God is passive and uninvolved in my life		
*	God expects me to be perfect		
*	God is demanding and rule-based		
+	God is a just judge		
#	God is too kind to punish people		
*	I can't meet God's standards		
*	God is often disappointed or displeased with me		
#	God is hands off and lenient		
+	I feel comfortable in God's presence		
#	I rarely feel like approaching God		
*	I need to work hard to be accepted by God		
*	God is not safe to approach		

+	God is merciful and kind		
+	I feel that God is dependable		
*	I am fearful of letting God be in total control of my life		
+	God is a God of grace		
#	God is a God of no precise rules or norms		
+	God is generous		
*	God is harsh and condemning		
#	Little reverence for God		
#	God doesn't seem to be in control of this world		
+	I feel safe letting God be in control of my life		
#	God is broad-minded		
+	I have a healthy respect for God		
#	God won't send anyone to hell		

View of God Results

Add up the number of each symbol that you placed a checkmark by on the previous page

Right now: As a Child:

* _____   * _____

+ _____   + _____

_____   # _____

1) This symbol * indicates a "Prescriptive View of God"
   This symbol + indicates a "Principial View of God"
   This symbol # indicates a "Permissive View of God"

2) Which View of God most characterized your perspective as a child? Prescriptive, Principial, or Permissive?

3) Which View of God most characterizes your perspective right now? Prescriptive, Principial, or Permissive?

4) Has your View of God changed since childhood? If so, how?

5) What surprised you the most about the results of your View of God?

Different Views of God

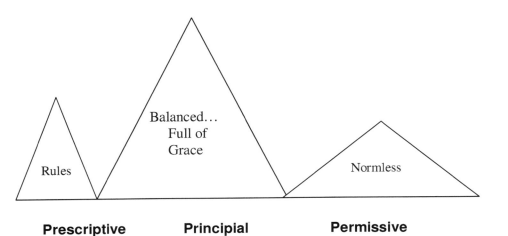

Prescriptive   **Principial**   **Permissive**

PRESCRIPTIVE – This view is usually founded on long standing customs with very little room for differences. It reduces beliefs to explicit rules or codes.

PRINCIPIAL – From this viewpoint principles are sufficiently abstract so that their application to a wide range of conduct is feasible without a violation of the principle. Values are unalterable, but methods can change.

PERMISSIVE – This view favors an extremely free and easy state of affairs with very few guidelines and norms.

Qualities that characterize God from three different Views of God

Prescriptive	Principial	Permissive
Authoritarian	Authoritative	Laissez-faire (hands-off)
Demanding	Disciplines in love	Doesn't discipline
Hard to Please	Steadfast	Noncommitted
Unapproachable	Trustworthy	Unreliable
Regimented	Accessible	Passive
Legalistic	Respectful	Normless
Demands Perfection	Forgiving	Lenient
Dogmatic	Honest	Noninterventionist
Strict	Adaptable	Unrestrained
Reserved	Relational	Unconnected
Based on Rules	Dependable	Unconcerned
Detailed	Fair	Broad-minded
Moralistic/Straight-laced	Full of Grace	Won't punish

Ways you might feel if you had this View of God?

Prescriptive	Principial	Permissive
Afraid of God	Healthy Fear and Respect for God	Disrespect for God
God is unapproachable	God is approachable	Rarely approach God
Avoids God's presence	Comfortable in God's presence	Not close to God
He's an angry Judge	He judges justly	He's too kind to punish me
I must be perfect	I am growing in His likeness	God is lenient
A relationship based on rules	A relationship of grace	God has no rules/norms

View of God According to Scripture

GOD IS AN INTEGRATED PERSON, not torn by love and justice.

Characteristic	Meaning	Scripture
Immutable	He never differs from himself; He changes not	Mal. 3:6
Infinite	He's Limitless	Ps. 147:5
Everlasting	No beginning, no end; time is different with God	Ps. 90:2
Omniscient	He possesses perfect knowledge	I Sam. 2:3 KJV
Omnipotent	He has all power, limitless	Rev. 19:6 KJV
Transcendent	He is exalted far above the created universe	Ps. 57:5
Faithful	He will always do what he says and will be true to His Word	Lam. 3:23
Good	Kind, benevolent, bestows blessings and shows loving kindness	Ps.27:13
Just	Righteous, but acts with justice	II Thess. 1:6
Omnipresent	God is everywhere present; always near us	Ps. 119:151
Infinite	His being knows no limits	Ps. 147:5
Merciful	Actively compassionate	Dan. 9:9
Gracious	God of grace; goodness of God	II Chron. 30:9
Love	Takes pleasure in, enjoys; active, creative, personal, intimate, and unconditional	Ps. 36:7
Holy	Infinite, incomprehensible; fullness of purity	Ps. 99:3, Isa. 6:3
Sovereign	He rules; Supreme	Isa. 40:10

Appendix B – Spiritual Formation Exercises

1. Lectio Divina [Prayer-filled Reading of the Scriptures]

- Silence – *Take several deep breaths and allow the silence to quiet the inside clutter*
- Read the Word – *Read a brief portion of Scripture, listening for a key phrase*
- Meditate – *Allow the Word to sink in from your head to your heart*
- Contemplate – *In solitude (place) and silence (close mouth) allow the text to work on you. Listen – what is God saying?*
- Action – *How is God prompting you to live out this passage?*

Group Lectio Divina

Here's a suggested outline for a Group Lectio Divina:

- Silence (silencio) - *Begin with a few moments of silence and then open with prayer.*
- Read the Word (lectio) - *The passage is read 2 or 3 times, slowly and deliberately. Participants are asked to choose a word that speaks to them and share it with the group.*
- Meditate (meditatio) - *Read the passage 2 or 3 times more (with a different voice). In silence, ask participants to reflect on the word or phrase that speaks to them, attending to the emotions, feelings, and meaning it brings up in them. Share these together in the group.*
- Contemplation (comtemplatio) - *Read the passage once or twice again (with a different voice); a period of silence is kept in order for each person to listen to what God is saying to them. Allow the participants to share what God is saying to them through the text.*

211

2. AEIOU #1

- A = Abide in Christ *(Spend time in silence focusing on God; offer him your heart & mind during this formation time)*
- E = Examine *(Using your senses, take in the scripture. Visualize the situation; Is there anything you see, smell, touch, or hear?)*
- I = I *(Personalize the scripture by putting your name in it; then read it out loud with your name in it)*
- Open your heart *(After reading the scripture, open your heart to God's Spirit, allowing him to speak to you personally)*
- U = Use *(How were you affected by this scripture today? How does God want you to apply it to your life? Pray back your response to God.)*

3. AEIOU #2

Read the scripture and then do the following:

- A = Ask questions
- E = Emphasize words *(Say the sentence a number of times, emphasizing different words each time)*
- I = Investigate *(Look for the answer to one or more of your questions)*
- O = Other scriptures *(Read some cross references/other scriptures about this subject)*
- U= Use it *(Make an application to your life)*

4. Praying the Scriptures [Madame Guyon]
Don't just skim the surface, plunge deeply within to grasp it all!

* Choose a passage that is simple & fairly practical *(This will usually be a small portion of Scripture.)*
* Come quietly and humble to the Lord *(Silence your heart.)*
* Read slowly the passage of Scripture. *(Meditate on the words and do not move from one line to another until you've sensed the heart of what you have read.)*
* Take a portion of the scripture that has touched you and turn it into a prayer *(Or turn each line into a prayer as you've sensed the heart of it.)*

5. P.R.A.Y. [A different way to pray]

* P – Praise God
* R – Repent of anything you've done recently that might have displeased God
* A – Admit that you need him
* Y – Yield to the Holy Spirit's control

6. Fifteen Minutes a Day with God

* Relax (One minute)   Be still and quiet and prepare your heart.
* Read (Four minutes) Pick a book of the Bible and read through it until the time is up OR pick a chapter or a few verses and read it over slowly several times.
* Reflect (Four minutes)   Pick out a verse or two from your reading and meditate on its meaning.
* Record (Two minutes)   What is God impressing upon your heart from this scripture?
* Request (Four minutes) Conclude your time in conversation to God (talking, listening, or in silence).

7. Spending Time with Christ [a Gospel Meditation]

A gospel meditation provides an opportunity for you to enter specific moments in Jesus' life & share his experience.

- Select a Gospel account of one event in the life of Christ.
- Begin with a brief prayer asking God to help you enter this story and encounter Jesus.
- Read the scripture slowly as you observe the situation presented.
- Watch, listen & stay attentive to Christ, not the other people in the story. *(Just be present to Jesus)*
- Don't try to analyze the story or learn its lessons. *(What did you discover about Jesus as you shared this experience with him?)*

8. Sitting in God's Presence or Centering Prayer
[A method by Basil Pennington]

- Simply shut your eyes and enjoy the presence of the Lord.
- Focus on Christ as he gazes back at you with his full loving attention and asks you to sit with him for a while.
- Gently return your attention to him by saying his name whenever you find your mind drifting to other things.

9. Breath Prayer [This combines the calming effect of breath with the words of Scripture.]

- Get seated comfortably and began slowly breathing.
- Begin inwardly saying a phrase of scripture in rhythm with your breathing. For instance:
  - Breathe in: "The Lord…"
  - Breathe out: "is my Shepherd"
- Focus during every repetition on the meaning of the words, praying them from the heart and in the heart.

214

10. Experiencing the Heart of God[434]

- Still your thoughts and emotions as you center your thoughts on Christ
- Meditate on a verse of scripture, saying it softly over & over to yourself until you can say it (or a portion of it) with your eyes closed. As you repeat the scripture allow yourself to see it with the eyes of your heart.
- Answer (or journal) your response to these questions
  - ✓ *What is the picture you see in your mind's eye as you repeat the scripture?*
  - ✓ *What does the scripture reveal about the heart of God?*
  - ✓ *Put yourself in the picture of this scripture in your mind. What is the Lord speaking to you personally as you see the truth of this scripture?*
- Take time to pray, saying to God what you have seen and heard from Him today through this experience.

11. Daily Examen [To increase your awareness of God]

- Take a few minutes to prayerfully review your day and what took place.
- Ask yourself these questions:
  - ✓ When did God feel closest to you today? When did he seem absent?
  - ✓ Ask forgiveness for any sin or ask another person to forgive you if needed. Thank God for his presence.

---

[434] Thom Gardner, *Healing the Wounded Heart* (Shippensburg, PA: Destiny Image Publishers, 2005).

Appendix C – Helpful Profiles

1) **The DISC insights Biblical Personality System** (The Institute for Motivational Living)
   - This profile helps you identify your behavior style – Dominant Driver, Influencing Inspiring, Compliant Correct, or Stable Steady.
   - Your pattern can include either 1, 2, or 3 of these behavior styles. The pattern name is compared to a particular bible character with that same pattern and some scriptures to study.)
   - See this website for more information: http://www.discinsights.com

2) **Houts Inventory of Spiritual Gifts** (The Leadership Centre Willow Creek
   - A profile that helps indicate your spiritual gifts

3) **Personal Patterns Predicting Infidelity**
   - This tool is available from a book by Dave Carder and gives you a score regarding your risk for an affair. It identifies family of origin issues and lifestyle patterns that make you more vulnerable to an affair.
   - Dave Carder, *Torn Asunder: Recovering from Extramarital Affairs.* (Chicago: Moody Press, 1995), 98-101.

4) **Inventory of Spiritual/Emotional Maturity**
   - This tool is available in a book by Peter Scazzero and scores you according to your general formation and discipleship. The score will place you in one of these levels of emotional maturity: emotional infant, child, adolescent, or adult.
   - Peter Scazzero, *The Emotionally Healthy Church: A Strategy for Discipleship that Actually Changes Lives* (Grand Rapids, MI: Zondervan, 2003), 60-66.

Appendix D - Holmes-Rahe Life Stress Inventory[435]

In the past 24 months, which of these events
have taken place in your life?
Circle the scores that apply to you;
then add up all your points to find your score.

Life Events	Score	Life Events	Score
Death of spouse	100	Son or daughter leaving home	29
Divorce	75	Trouble with in-laws	29
Martial separation	65	Outstanding personal achievement	28
Jail term or other institution	63	Spouse begins or stops work	26
Death of close family member	63	Begin or end formal schooling	26
Personal injury or illness	53	Change in living conditions	25
Marriage	50	Revision of personal habits	24
Fired at work	47	Trouble with boss	23
Marital reconciliation	45	Change in work hours or conditions	20
Retirement	45	Change in residence	20
Change in health or behavior of a family member	44	Change in schools	20
Pregnancy	40	Change in type or amount of recreation	19
Sexual Difficulties	39	Change in church	19

---

[435] Thomas Holmes and Richard Rahe, "Holmes-Rahe Social Readjustment Rating Scale," *Journal of Psychosomatic Research* 11 (1967): 213-218.

		activity	
Gained a new family member	39	Change in social activities	18
Business readjustment	39	Taking on a loan	17
Change in financial state	38	Change in sleeping habits	16
Death of close friend	37	Change in number of family get-togethers	15
Change to different line of work	36	Change in eating habits	15
Change in number of arguments with spouse	35	Vacation	13
Taking on a mortgage	31	Holidays/Christmas alone	12
Foreclosure of mortgage or loan	30	Minor violations of the law	11
Change in responsibilities at work	29	**TOTAL**	

Less than 150 points: relatively low amount of life change and low susceptibility to stress-induced health breakdown in the next two years

150 to 300 points: implies 50% chance of a major health breakdown in the next two years

More than 300 points: implies 80% chance of a major health breakdown in the next two years.